"This excellent and highly accessible book deals with its uncomfortable subject—rejection—with sensitivity and nuance. No matter where we stand on the Christological issues addressed in the New Testament, we will all recognize the range of responses discussed in this book, including hurt, anger, and disappointment, and we may all learn that rejection can also be a catalyst for positive change and growth."

—ADELE REINHARTZ, professor of classics and religious studies, University of Ottawa

"As a preacher and pastor, I so appreciate the clarity, accessibility and wisdom in Bill Loader's skillful analysis of early Christian communities' responses to rejection—their own and the rejection Jesus experienced in his ministry and execution. Loader explicates the differences between responses to rejection that risk hate, violence and exclusion, in contrast to responses that sustain divine love, forgiveness and belonging, as seen in Jesus' life and death, as central to covenant faith, and from the heart of Divine being. In a time when many voices cry vengeance and hatred, this book digs down into the soil of scripture, to open up space for cultivating anew Christian compassion and justice."

—NANCY VICTORIN-VANGERUD, adjunct professor, United Theological Seminary of the Twin Cities

"William Loader is a master of scientific New Testament exegesis. At the same time, he can write not only for specialists, but also for interested lay people. His book is a very readable introduction to questions of NT interpretation (esp. the Gospels, Paul, and Hebrews) and the context in which these questions were and are relevant. Loader's book is also an introduction to the way the parables and sayings of Jesus developed, and were interpreted, before they became part of New Testament writings. In our times, where religious thought is under pressure, it is very welcome to reassure believers in their belief, and to make non-believers curious to get more knowledge about biblical issues."

—WOLFGANG KRAUS, professor emeritus, Saarland University

"This book takes a fresh look at scripture through the practical lens of ordinary people coping with grief borne out of rejection. It is creative in how it discerns resources in the biblical text to tease out our myriad responses to this universal and perpetual human emotion. It challenges us to think of our own responses to both rejection and acceptance, and it encourages us to position ourselves with the healthiest of gospel responses — while also enhancing awareness of unhealthy responses. But this book's real gold is that it gives us the opportunity to once again refine our Christian faith into a transformative faith of love, life and abundant generosity."

—ROSALIE CLARKE MACLARTY, chaplain, Knox Grammar School, New South Wales

"The theme of rejection is one that has received relatively little attention in contemporary Christian writing. With the deftness born of a lifetime of study and teaching, Bill Loader brings this theme into the foreground to take the reader on a journey of rediscovering what we thought we knew. In three movements, Loader first sets out how early followers of Jesus came to terms with people rejecting their belief and message. He then places Jesus in the context of Jewish and Roman hopes and gives a fresh and nuanced account of the significance that early writers gave to the death of Jesus. In the final movement, Loader gives a coherent and compelling account of the inner logic of the Good News, calling out superficial answers and showing love to be at the heart of it all. This book holds up a mirror to us as readers to notice how we make sense of the Christian story; it offers a challenging journey with an expert guide!"

—VICKY BALABANSKI, Uniting College for Leadership and Theology, University of Divinity, South Australia

Facing Rejection

Facing Rejection

Responses
in the New Testament Writings

WILLIAM LOADER

CASCADE *Books* • Eugene, Oregon

FACING REJECTION
Responses in the New Testament Writings

Copyright © 2025 William Loader. All rights reserved. Except for brief quotations in critical publications or reviews, no part of this book may be reproduced in any manner without prior written permission from the publisher. Write: Permissions, Wipf and Stock Publishers, 199 W. 8th Ave., Suite 3, Eugene, OR 97401.

Cascade Books
An Imprint of Wipf and Stock Publishers
199 W. 8th Ave., Suite 3
Eugene, OR 97401

www.wipfandstock.com

PAPERBACK ISBN: 979-8-3852-2792-1
HARDCOVER ISBN: 979-8-3852-2793-8
EBOOK ISBN: 979-8-3852-2794-5

Cataloguing-in-Publication data:

Names: Loader, William, author

Title: Facing rejection : responses in the New Testament writings / William Loader.

Description: Eugene, OR: Cascade Books, 2025 | Includes bibliographical references and index.

Identifiers: ISBN 979-8-3852-2792-1 (paperback) | ISBN 979-8-3852-2793-8 (hardcover) | ISBN 979-8-3852-2794-5 (ebook)

Subjects: LCSH: Rejection (Psychology)—Religious aspects. |Bible—New Testament—Criticism, interpretation, etc.

Classification: BF575.R35 L63 2025 (paperback) | BF575.R35 (ebook)

06/20/25

Contents

	Preface	vii
1	Dealing with Rejection	1
2	Coping with the Rejection of Jesus	46
3	Coping with Acceptance, Healthily and Otherwise	87
	Concluding Reflections	105

Preface

"I hate you! Why don't you love me?"

This book is about grief, or, more particularly, about the grief of facing rejection and responses to this grief in the writings of the New Testament. Some, I suggest, are healthy, and some are unhealthy. The grief of rejection hurts, especially where you have something invested in the relationship with the person rejecting you. This can be in individual relationships where you hope for and expect love but find rejection. The pain can be hard to bear and sometimes lead to hate and even violence toward the person we want to love and who we want to love us.

In the New Testament writings, we are mostly not dealing with rejection in close interpersonal relationships, but we do see reflection on the pain of rejection. It is not difficult to imagine how it would have been when in a close-knit Jewish community one member offers what she claims to be good news, only to be shunned or refused. We have this sometimes referred to as happening in families, such as in the saying, "One's foes will be members of one's own household" (Matt 10:36). If your faith matters to you and you are claiming to promote what that faith has now come to mean, then rejection of that claim will not be easy to take.

At one level, proclaiming good news to strangers, especially non-Jews, gentiles, in a foreign land, would mean you would face rejection and that would be easier to accept. Rejection by fellow Jews would be another story. The same would apply if you, yourself, were a gentile and had converted to Judaism before joining the

Preface

Jesus movement, but also if you were a gentile convert to the Jesus movement and had embraced its claim to be the faithful bearer of Israel's tradition and Jews were rejecting that claim.

Such rejection of your "good news" as not good news at all would not only hurt. It would also potentially have you question your own existence: have you got it wrong? You might have to address such self-doubts, including by identifying and dealing not only with what you understand lies behind the rejection but also really why you think you are right.

The first generations of the Jesus movement, which morphed over time into the church and Christianity, clearly had to grapple with rejection, and this book will show how they did so in a range of different ways, some of them helpful, some of them arguably unhelpful and even harmful. And all of this had an impact on the subsequent history of the movement and the wider community. The first chapter of this book will explore these responses.

Rejection was not unprecedented. The most dramatic and humiliating rejection occurred at the very center of the story they told, Jesus' crucifixion. Crucifixion was designed to shame and humiliate. It was a crude deterrent. How could they hail as their hero one who had been put to death so shamefully, executed even by officials of the Roman Empire in which you lived? Belief in his resurrection did not alter the fact that Jesus faced rejection and that there was a need to come to terms with it. The pain was also far more than just the gruesomeness of the means of execution. It was the pain of hope rejected, the dashing of expectations. The second chapter explores ways in which the early generations sought to come to terms with Jesus' death.

The book concludes by turning the theme of rejection upside down and reflecting on the challenge of coming to terms with acceptance and how hard it can be to open oneself to receive love, how even then, responses can sometimes be anything but calm: "I hate you! I don't want you to love me! I'm okay as I am!" For some, being loved is experienced as a serious threat, from which they prefer to hide and run away and if it comes too close, to seek to terminate it.

Preface

Underlying the theme of this book are a number of studies I have conducted in recent years, dealing especially with the theme of rejection. They include, "Dissent and Disparagement: Dealing with Conflict and the Pain of Rejection in the Gospel according to John," in William R. G. Loader, *Christology, Soteriology and Ethics in John and Hebrews: Collected Essays*, WUNT 478 (Tübingen: Mohr Siebeck, 2022), 263–78—first published in *HTS Teologiese Studies/Theological Studies* 77 (2), a6570. https://doi.org/10.4102/hts.v77i2.6570; "Processing Rejection in Christian Beginnings," *Festschrift for Stelian Tofana. Sacra Scripta. Journal of the Centre for Biblical Studies 21.1–2* (2023), 69–86; "Forgiveness Monopoly? Identity Formation and Demarcation in the Jesus Movement," in William Loader, *Jesus Left Loose Ends: Collected Essays* (Adelaide: ATF, 2021), 281–95; and "Rationalising Rejection in John 8 and Elsewhere in the Fourth Gospel," in *Revelation and Conflict in John 7 and 8. Historical, Literary, and Theological Readings from the Colloquium Ioanneum 2023 in Vienna* (WUNT; ed. R. Alan Culpepper and Jörg Frey; Tübingen: Mohr Siebeck, 2024).

Issues of dealing with rejection, dissent, and difference recur constantly throughout history, and have in recent years sadly again received prominence within the human community. My hope is that this book will make some small contribution towards finding alternative ways to live together with difference.

The reflections in this book will be close to home for many, because they touch on common human experience, while at the same time being moments and emphases that have brought both goodness and harm to our world. They are offered in the hope that those who bear our precious faith traditions will be helped to discern what brings life and hope in them from what does not.

Biblical texts cited in this book are in the NRSV translation unless indicated by an asterisk where, as author, I have offered my own translation in the interests of rendering a more literal translation.

This book had its beginnings in a series I offered recently in Perth, designed to encourage insights and discussion of core issues in contemporary faith. I dedicate this book to all who seek

Preface

peace and hope in the midst of dealing with conflict and dissent. I want especially to thank Reverend Alan and Sharyn Robinson, and Gisela, my wife, who read an earlier draft of the book and exposed typos, frowned at long sentences, and offered encouraging comments.

William Loader

1

Dealing with Rejection

DEALING WITH REJECTION IN MARK

We are fortunate to have accounts of Jesus' ministry passed down to us in the form of "Gospels." The word *gospel* simply meant "good news" and could refer to any message, long or short, purporting to be good news. Israel's tradition used it to designate messages of hope when finally, God would reign, as reflected in the words,

> How beautiful upon the mountains are the feet of the messenger who announces peace, who brings good news, who announces salvation, who says to Zion, "Your God reigns." (Isa 52:7)

Roman emperors could use "good news" of themselves and their achievements in bringing peace, safe roads, and seaways. It belonged to their language of propaganda. Mark uses it of his extended story of Jesus' ministry (1:1), and so such extended accounts like his came to be called "Gospels"; hence, the word *gospel* became also a term for a special kind of writing.

Mark's Gospel, like the accounts of famous people written at the time, ancient biographies, draws on sources and traditions passed on over the four decades since Jesus. But is written not primarily to satisfy the curiosity of the historian, but to bring out the significance of Jesus to people of his own day. Therefore, we are dealing with more than just history. We are dealing with creativity and imagination designed to move the hearer to a response of faith.

The Parable of the Sower

Very early in his account Mark brings in chapter 4 a collection of parables that in part deal with rejection. They will have originated with Jesus and are typical of the artistry of his message. They will have been told and retold, reflected upon and expanded over the four decades before Mark used them. The first of these in Mark deals with rejection, though that is not its primary focus. If anything, it is incidental.

> "Listen. A sower went out to sow seed. 4 And while he was sowing, some seed fell beside the path and the birds came and ate it. 5 Others fell on stony ground where there wasn't much soil, and it came up straightaway because there was no depth of soil 6 but when the sun came up, it was scorched and having no root, it dried up. 7 And others fell among thorns and the thorns came up and strangled it and it did not produce any grain. 8 And others fell on good soil and were productive, coming up and growing to end up producing a harvest, some a threefold yield, some a sixtyfold and some a hundredfold." 9 And he added: "Whoever has ears, listen!" (Mark 4:3–9)*

When Jesus first told the parable, some of those listening will very likely have been wheat farmers. Galilee was, after all, the breadbasket of the region. They would know what he was talking about. It was typical of Jesus to use the very familiar. Wheat farmers listening would be nodding their heads. Yes, you scatter the wheat and of course the birds will take some and some will land in soil with little depth, and some will end up competing with lots of weeds . . . all very familiar. But you do it because you know that a miracle comes at the end. Some grows up healthily and produces heads of wheat and then it's soon harvest time. Jesus' image has an impressively large harvest, probably larger than most would have expected.

"So what?" they might have asked. If they had been listening, they might have made the connection to Jesus' message; the kingdom, the reign of God really will come. You can believe it! Yes, despite the setbacks, it will come! Others before him had used the imagery of harvest to speak about hope and that will have been familiar to some. The chance that some will have got the point of the parable was very high. Focus on the hope, despite the setbacks, despite rejections! Yes, that's what we farmers do.

That was a simple enough message of hope and not unlike other parables Jesus tells in the same chapter. Farmers sow seed not really knowing how it all works (4:26–29), but it does! Don't be put off by small beginnings. Think of the tiny mustard seed. Let it grow and it will become a large shrub (4:30–32).

People listening to Mark's Gospel would have heard more in the story. Yes, it reflected Jesus' positive approach as he began his ministry in Galilee, but they knew there was more to come, more than just setbacks.

It is not difficult to imagine that the simple parable of the sower generated more reflection over the years before Mark. Perhaps Jesus and his disciples talked about it more. Mark suggests they did, but what he brings in 4:13–20 clearly reflects thoughts that will have arisen when people reflected on the parable in a church context where, for instance, they faced persecution. In that sense, Mark moves beyond history to portray Jesus as expounding its significance for that later church setting.

> Then he addresses them saying, "You don't get this parable? Then how will you get any of the parables? 14 The sower sows the word. 15 Those by the wayside where the seed was sown are the people who, when they hear, immediately Satan comes and removes the word sown into them. 16 Those sown on stony ground are the people who, when they hear the word, immediately receive it with joy, 17 but have no root in themselves and are short-lived and when persecution troubles hit them because of the word, immediately they stumble and fall. 18

Facing Rejection

> And others sown among thorn bushes, these are people who hear the word 19 but worries about this life and the deceitfulness of wealth and greed for other things come in and choke the word and they fail to produce a harvest. 20 And those sown on good soil are those who hear the word, take it on board, and produce a harvest, some thirtyfold, some sixtyfold, some a hundredfold." (Mark 4:13–20)*

As we read that exposition, we can see that the focus now falls not on the wonderful climax, but on the problems in the interim, namely forms of rejection. Saying that the birds snapping up the grain are like Satan stopping people from responding is simple enough, but the other explanations seem more to be addressing why some members who did respond and joined the church later abandoned their faith. Some did so when persecution came, like the seed with no depth of soil. Some did so when other priorities such as greed for wealth took over, like the seeds among the weeds.

This creative reworking would have helped people in early faith communities come to terms with why not everyone who joined them stayed, why some gave up. Understanding why it is that some people reject can help with the experience of facing rejection. At the same time the exposition may well have served at the time as a challenge to listeners, themselves, not to give up and so to be aware of the dangers that could lead to abandoning one's faith.

It is very likely that this exposition of the parable of the sower, using it to explain why people reject their faith, was already part of the collection of seed parables that Mark received as an oral tradition. He had earlier used such a collection of stories in 2:1—3:6, depicting Jesus in controversies. It was easier to remember stories together with similar themes as they were passed on by word of mouth.

Part of Mark's task was to weave all these clusters of traditions together in his Gospel into a sequence that made sense. He had no detailed CV of Jesus, nor did the other Gospel writers, which is why they felt quite free at times to change Mark's sequence of events and tell his stories differently.

Dealing with Rejection

We can see Mark's hand in the verses that immediately follow the initial telling of the parable. He has Jesus' disciples ask him about the parables. The answer he has Jesus give seems very strange, especially if we understand telling parables as a means of communication.

> And when he was on his own, those who were with him along with the twelve asked him about the parables 11 and he told them, "The mystery of the kingdom of God is given to you, but for those outside everything comes in parables, 12 'so that seeing, they may not really see and have insight, and hearing, they may not really hear and have understanding, lest they turn and be forgiven.'" (Mark 4:11–12, citing Isa 6:10)*

Mark makes the extraordinary claim that Jesus told parables so that people would not understand. He has Jesus quote Isaiah 6 to underline the claim, where the prophet reports what he heard as God's instruction:

> And he said, "Go and say to this people: 'Keep listening, but do not comprehend; keep looking, but do not understand.' 10 Make the mind of this people dull, and stop their ears, and shut their eyes, so that they may not look with their eyes, and listen with their ears, and comprehend with their minds, and turn and be healed." (Isa 6:9–10)

To wrap up his presentation of Jesus' seed parables, Mark repeats the claim that Jesus spoke to the crowds only in parables but explained everything to his disciples (4:33–34).

> With many such parables he spoke his message to them as much as they could listen to. 34 He did not address them except in parables, but in private he explained everything to his own disciples. (Mark 4:33–34)*

These comments given to Jesus by Mark in 4:10–12 and 33–34 appear to turn the role of parables on their head. Instead of being a creative means of communication, they deliberately obscure and do so in the interest of making certain that outsiders do not understand. Citing the passage from Isaiah goes even further by implying that this was God's intention.

At worst, Mark's hearers might congratulate themselves as being the privileged insiders and feel smug about looking down on those chosen by God to be outsiders. For some, this may have given them comfort as they faced rejection, perhaps with the sense of relief that it was "meant to be." This might relieve their stress but in terms of human community it is far from healthy, effectively writing off some people as destined not to belong. And it stands in tension with understandings of God as generous and loving towards all.

We shall find other instances of such strategies of explanation employed by other New Testament writers. At one level it suggests a closed system. Some are insiders and some are deliberately destined to be outsiders and will always be so. Pressed to its logical conclusion it could make any effort to persuade outsiders to repent a meaningless and hopeless enterprise. Their fate is not to believe. God has determined it. That would then raise the question whether, if that is so, they should carry any blame, let alone be punished.

In reality, this was not a closed system. It was a way of dealing with rejection that we find also in Jewish literature of the time, for instance in the writings of the Jewish sect found among the documents discovered last century in caves by the Dead Sea. They spoke of children of light and children of darkness, as determined by God, but the categories were not water-tight. You could become a child of the light, a chosen and elect person, by changing your mind. So, far from implying that those who reject bore no guilt for their response because it was all part of God's plan, the assumption is that they are held accountable, and, more than that, could turn and become insiders. Indeed, it is likely that the language of being chosen or not chosen served to persuade rather than to reject or cope with rejection, though that was also part of its function. It sounded like a closed system, but it was anything but a closed system. It clearly leaked.

Thus, the rhetoric of saying "it was meant to be" was at one level a rhetorical fiction designed to bring comfort in the face of

Dealing with Rejection

rejection, but in most instances where we find it, never meant to stand in the way of God's goodness and offer of forgiveness. There was always wriggle room, room for change.

Parables were a characteristic way in which Jesus taught and the purpose was not to prevent but to promote understanding. At best, Mark may be playing with the way parables work. They are not explanations; they are images that work differently from explanations. They are like metaphors that on the surface make no sense, such as when someone says, "She's an encyclopedia." People have to make the jump from what is at first sight nonsense to the idea being evoked: she is very well informed about many things or such like. In a similar way with parables, the meaning is not immediately obvious until the penny drops, so to speak, the "aha" moment, where we say: "Oh, I see! I get it!" Parables work if you are willing to make the connection, to get their hidden or secret meaning. They don't if you aren't.

Mark's insiders, the twelve as well as those with them, get the secret. "Secret" or "mystery" was a word often used to speak about hope, how God would act in the future. There was an element of the unknown in relation to exactly how God would act ("mystery" is appropriate), but it was no secret that God would act. Mark speaks of "the mystery of the kingdom of God." The "how" was not defined, but the faith that God would act, God would reign, was proclaimed far and wide.

Those who responded to the challenge to turn to God and believe this good news became in that sense insiders. Mark may appear to be saying that the insiders were always guaranteed to understand everything because Jesus explained it to them, as Mark explains in 4:33–34. He illustrates Jesus' giving such explanations with his report of the parable's meaning in 4:13–20, where it is applied to church situations. We soon find out, however, as we go through Mark, that the disciples' understanding was far from adequate. In fact, at one point Mark has Jesus allude to the same passage from Isaiah to complain about their failure to see his meaning.

> Why are you talking about not having bread? Don't you yet realize and get the point? Do you have closed minds?

> 18 As they say, "with eyes but not looking, with ears but not hearing"? (Mark 8:17–18)*

Instead, as the Gospel narrative proceeds, Mark depicts the disciples as increasingly dense, almost certainly as a way of challenging people of his own day to be more perceptive. They end up betraying, denying, and running away! At least, the men do.

We have, therefore, to be cautious about taking Mark too literally both in what he says about the disciples' private instruction and what he says about parables and outsiders. While he does use the "it was meant to be" rhetoric in Mark 4, he clearly does not let it govern his thinking as reflected in the rest of the Gospel. Nowhere else does Mark suggest that rejection is predetermined by God and certainly, Mark, like others using such language, does not see it as a closed system that relieves those who reject of any responsibility or prevents them from changing their minds and accepting the gospel.

That caution is evident in Matthew's retelling of this part of Mark. He changes Jesus' response from "but for those outside everything comes in parables, 12 'so that seeing, they may not really see and have insight, and hearing, they may not really hear and have understanding, lest they turn and be forgiven'" (Mark 4:11–12)* to "The reason I speak to them in parables is because 'seeing they do not perceive . . .'" (Matt 13:13).* Thus Matthew removes the notion of telling parables in order that people may not understand and replaces it by using the allusion to Isaiah as a way of explaining that some do not respond positively and implying they, not God, are to blame.

Dealing with Rejection in the Rest of Mark

One of the earliest references to rejection reaches very likely right back to the setting of Jesus' ministry, or at least to the context in Galilee. Mark reports that in sending out disciples two by two they were to expect to be put up by locals as they traveled about Galilee, but also to be rejected. He then reports Jesus saying:

Dealing with Rejection

> And whatever place does not welcome you or want to hear you, leave them and shake the dust off your feet as evidence against them. (Mark 6:11)*

This reflects very early days, perhaps quite literally a sending out of disciples by Jesus, as Mark suggests, or at least very early in the movement when itinerancy was still the pattern. It does not tell us much more than that rejection was to be expected and, in that sense, accepted. Let it be. Shake the dust off your feet and move on. But there is more: the saying speaks of that shaking off the dust as evidence, probably understood as saying God will judge you for this rejection. Certainly, this is how Matthew and Luke read it (Matt 10:14-15; Luke 9:5; 10:10-12). The instruction matches Jesus' own response to rejection in his hometown synagogue (6:1-6). He acknowledged the rejection, as to be expected, and then moved on.

As we review other parts of Mark, we also find ourselves operating at two levels: what Mark is doing and what might lie behind Mark and potentially reflect responses of Jesus. We have already noted the collection of five controversy stories that Mark inherited and that we now find in 2:1—3:6. They depict Jesus facing critics and responding to rejection with argument in the form of his distinctive two-liner quips.

It is highly probable that the earliest form of the anecdotes reflects a real encounter between Jesus and his critics and that Jesus' original response thus took the form of a clever two-part saying, typical of his responses in similar anecdotes elsewhere. When criticized, for instance, for saying to the man let down through the roof, "Your sins are forgiven," Jesus responds: "What is easier, to say to the paralyzed man, 'Your sins are forgiven' or to say, 'Get up and take your stretcher and walk'?" (2:9).* Telling a lame person to get up and walk is at one level much harder, but for the critics, declaring God's forgiveness is the problem.

These stories will have been told and retold over the forty years before Mark and, as with the parables in Mark 4, they will have been shaped, trimmed, and supplemented in the process. It continues after Mark where we can see how Matthew, for instance, both trims and expands them. (We return to this below.) It is sometimes difficult to know what might already have been added before Mark and what Mark himself will have added.

In the stories as Mark now retells them, there is also an overlay that supplements Jesus' arguments, his clever two-part responses, with assertions of Jesus' authority, perhaps added by Mark. Thus, for instance, after Jesus' quip, "What is easier, to say to the paralyzed man, 'Your sins are forgiven' or to say, 'Get up and take your stretcher and walk'?" (2:9), we read "But so that you may know that the Son of Man has authority on earth to forgive sins"—he says to the paralyzed man— 11 "I tell you, get up, pick up your stretcher and go back home" (2:11).* And following the quip, "The Sabbath was made for human beings not human beings for the Sabbath" (2:27)* we read "So the Son of Man is master also of the Sabbath" (2:28).*

Calling Jesus Son of Man identified him with a figure of Jewish expectation who would exercise God's judgement at the end of time and who therefore had authority to declare what was law and what was not. In the story of the man let down through the roof (2:1–12), Mark probably also added blasphemy to the critics' charge, thereby foreshadowing the accusation of blasphemy that would surface at Jesus' trial before the Sanhedrin (14:63–64) and would surface in trials in Mark's own time, and at the same time exposing it as flawed because Jesus was not claiming to forgive sins on his own authority in place of God.

These additions fit also the way Mark is contrasting Jesus' authority in interpreting Scripture with that of the scribes who are confronting him. In the first public scene of Jesus ministry Mark introduces the theme of authority and Jesus' new approach.

> People were astounded at his teaching because he was teaching them with authority and not like the scribes. (1:22)*

> And everyone was amazed and started to ask themselves, "What is this? New teaching with authority." (1:27)*

Dealing with Rejection

Matthew takes the stories over from Mark and expands them by adding material. It also looks very likely that Mark will have already added material and that others had also done so before him. It is never possible to know for sure what might have happened, so that we can speak only of what is likely to have happened, given how we see such anecdotes treated subsequently.

Jesus' response to rejection in 2:1–12 was a clever reply. We find him making a similarly clever reply when in the next anecdote he faces criticism for being willing to dine with tax collectors like Levi, whom he invited to follow him, and sinners (2:13–17): "The sick need a doctor, not the well" (2:17).* He was thereby putting response to human need ahead of fears of being contaminated by keeping bad company. Again, what follows was probably an addition asserting Jesus' authority: "I came not to call righteous people but sinners" (2:17).* When he retells the story, Matthew reinforces what he rightly sees as Jesus' approach when he has Jesus precede his reply with the comment: "Go and learn what this means: 'I desire compassion not sacrifice'" (9:9, citing Hosea 6:6).

The third anecdote about fasting contrasts the behavior of Jesus and his disciples with that of the followers of John the Baptist and the Pharisees (2:18–22). You don't fast at a wedding celebration: "The bridegroom's men can't fast while the bridegroom is with them" (2:19). Jesus was using the imagery of the wedding feast, a common image of hope, to say: hope is here, breaking in already through what I am doing.

It is very likely that those who looked back on what was to follow then added: one day they will fast, when he is taken from them through crucifixion (2:20). It is probably Mark who then adds the sayings about the incompatibility of new wine and old wineskins and new patches on old garments. It picks up and reinforces his theme of Jesus' teaching as new, with an authority unlike that of the scribes, as in 1:27, cited above.

The fourth anecdote reports how Jesus' disciples plucked some heads of wheat as they walked through the wheat field on a Sabbath day and ate them, a casual, harmless act, but one which evoked protests from some rather extreme critics. Jesus' two-liner

Facing Rejection

response is telling: "The Sabbath was made for human beings not human beings for the Sabbath" (2:27).* In other words, the focus of biblical law, indeed God's focus, is human well-being not the keeping of rules. While Jesus' response is an argument, Mark overlays it, as he had in the story of the healing of the paralytic, with another reference to Jesus' authority as the Son of Man: "So the Son of Man is master also of the Sabbath" (2:28),* as he had in 2:12.

Conflict over liberal attitudes towards the Sabbath must have kept coming up in the early years of the Jesus movement. From this time probably comes the supplementary argument in 2:25–26 about David and his companions, who when they were hungry, were permitted to eat bread reserved by law for the priests (1 Sam 21:1–7), which it dates to the time when Abiathar was high priest. This somewhat changes the issue from people idly plucking and chewing grain on the Sabbath to their doing so because they were hungry, providing some justification.

Whoever added it did not realize that the reference to Abiathar was a mistake. He was not the high priest at the time. Matthew and Luke recognized the mistake and so dropped the reference. Interestingly, Matthew supplements the argument further by having Jesus point out that priests work on the Sabbath and then summing up what he rightly saw as Jesus' stance by again having him cite Hosea 6:6, "But if you had known what this means, 'I desire compassion and not sacrifice,' you would not have condemned the innocent" (Matt 12:7). Matthew brought the first three of Mark's controversy anecdotes together in Matthew 9, but kept the fourth and fifth until Matthew 12, which served his storyline better.

The fifth and final anecdote of the collection of controversies in Mark shows similar levels of meaning. Jesus makes his typical terse provocative response: "Is it lawful to do good or do harm on the Sabbath?" (3:4).* His critics could have said: "Come back and heal him tomorrow! That way you will avoid working on the Sabbath." Jesus' priority lies elsewhere and he claims that he reflects God's priority: people matter most, more than keeping Sabbath.

Again, we find an overlay, probably added by Mark, who has Jesus continue: "To save life or to kill" (3:4).* That went beyond the issue in the scene to point forward to what the critics would then go on to do: namely to collaborate with the local Herodian authorities to seek to kill Jesus (3:6). This way Mark connects the critics to those who eventually brought about Jesus' crucifixion. Matthew, again, makes additions, to add further justification for Jesus' action as in conformity with the Law, when he cites how it was permissible to rescue a sheep stuck in a hole on the Sabbath (12:12), a saying which Luke preserves in a different context (14:5).

Underlying each of these anecdotes is an image of Jesus meeting critique and rejection with counter-argument in the form of a clever provocative quip. We can see evidence also of attempts to bolster Jesus' response with supplementary argument, particularly evident in Matthew's additions. A consistent addition likely to derive from Mark is countering the objection by asserting Jesus' status, especially his authority as Son of Man. The stories appear to go right back to the time of Jesus and reflect his distinctive style of discourse. Later generations listening to them might generalize from the depiction of the critics who in part reflect extreme positions to assuming such responses were typical of all Jews and so have them serve less healthy attitudes.

Divine Reassurance in Mark

Mark's Gospel offers reassurance to believers facing possible rejection and opposition not only by appealing to Jesus' status and authority but also by reports of divine confirmation. We see this already in the first chapter, where Mark depicts Jesus as affirmed by God's own voice in the declaration from heaven at Jesus' baptism, a declaration only to Jesus but, in its being reported, serving Mark's story as an announcement to all listening to his Gospel.

> And just as he was coming up out of the water, he saw the heavens torn apart and the Spirit descending like a dove on him. 11 And a voice came from heaven, "You are my beloved Son. With you I am well pleased." (Mark 1:11)*

Facing Rejection

We have a similar declaration at his transfiguration, but there a public one, instructing the disciples therefore to listen to him: "This is my beloved Son. Listen to him!" (9:7),* a pertinent instruction after the author has had Jesus confront his disciples in 8:17-18 for not doing so and in the context of his seeking in vain to persuade them of his priorities of servant leadership in Mark 8—10.

Mark underlines Jesus' status also by highlighting his ability to exorcise demons and heal (1:32-34; 3:7-12; 6:53-56), and to perform miraculous acts on nature, such as stilling a storm (4:35-41), walking on water (6:45-52), and multiplying food (6:30-44; 8:1-10). These nature miracles also evoke and are inspired by stories from Israel's past, such as the parting of the sea at the exodus of Israel from Egypt and their being fed by manna in the wilderness. Such stories reassure Mark's listeners not only about Jesus' status and power but also about the fact that he and therefore they stand in continuity with Israel's past.

The appeal to Israel's tradition also includes seeing in it a precedent for rejection of God's agents, the prophets, both in what happened to Jesus and in what they, themselves, may be experiencing. That comes to a climax in Mark's account of Jesus' final days in Jerusalem, in which he foretells the temple's destruction, an event of very recent history for Mark's listeners, and depicts the destruction as God's judgement on those who rejected Jesus.

Mark's version of Jesus' parable of the workers in the vineyard draws on traditional imagery to depict Jesus as in line with the prophets of old, represented as the vineyard owner's messengers sent to gather the grape harvest (12:1-11). In a retrospect on Jesus' life, Mark has Jesus depicted as like the owner's loved Son who faced rejection and death. Mark completes his version with an allusion to Jesus' vindication by resurrection and the creation of a new temple comprising Jesus' faithful followers, a reassurance also to Mark's own listeners. Mark has Jesus cite Scripture to declare in reassurance:

> What will the master of the vineyard do? He will come and destroy those tenants and give the vineyard to others. 10 Have you not read the scripture, "The stone which the

Dealing with Rejection

builders rejected had become the cornerstone; 11 this is the Lord's doing and it is marvelous in our eyes"? (Mark 12:9–11, citing Ps 118:22–23)*

Mark was doing more than offering reassurance to his listeners facing rejection or potential rejection, but offering such reassurance was certainly part of his agenda. They can take comfort in their faith that God affirmed their Jesus, that his actions were in continuity with God's actions in the past and proved his divine power, and that God judged those who rejected Jesus and vindicated him by resurrection.

They could be assured they were on the right track and more than that: they were now the legitimate replacement for the temple. Mark has Jesus falsely accused at his trial of declaring he would destroy the temple: "We heard him say, 'I will destroy this temple, made with hands'" (14:58),* but the positive part of that accusation was clearly true as Mark portrays it: "and in three days I will build another, not made with hands."* Mark wants his listeners not only to know that rejection of Jesus led to God's judgement, including the destruction of the temple prefigured in Jesus' cursing of the fig tree for not bearing fruit (11:12–14, 20–21) and predicted in Mark 13. He wants them to know that they are the new temple.

Mark, therefore, brings a range of responses to rejection. In our next chapter we will look more closely at how Mark dealt with the rejection of Jesus, especially because of his death, but already we have seen that Mark uses Jesus' conflicts as a model for dealing with the conflicts and rejections that his listeners would face. These include Jesus' recognition, as expressed in the parable of the Sower, that some rejection was inevitable. They include also his response to criticism with argument, in the form of his clever two-line responses. Clearly in subsequent retellings these quips have received supplementary argument.

For Mark, however, the focus has mainly shifted from argument that might help his listeners hear what grounded Jesus' response, and has come to focus on Jesus' status. That included depictions of heavenly affirmation, evidence of divinely empowered miracles, demonstrating ability to expel demons, heal the sick, and defy natural limitations to change weather and multiply food. These not only reassured Mark's listeners that their faith in who Jesus was was well grounded, but that it was also in harmony with Israel's faith of old since his miraculous acts echoed miracles in Israel's ancient story. Claims that their faith in Jesus put them at odds with Israel's faith were to be refuted.

Mark's listeners would also find solace in being reminded that their rejection mirrored Jesus' rejection and the rejection of the prophets of old. They would find solace in being helped to see themselves as indeed part of God's plan, to be God's temple not made with hands. In that sense they could see themselves as chosen, for which Mark could then employ the language of predestination in declaring, on the one hand, that they were the chosen elect, but that those who rejected them, on the other hand, were destined to do so.

This was a dangerous notion when pressed both for its implications for how they approached God and for how they approached dissent. It could indeed portray God as selectively loving some and being of the opposite nature towards others and destining some for eternal damnation. Its logic wobbles seriously because total determinism would have to absolve the damned of all responsibility and therefore all blame. Like those who have used such language before him, Mark does not press it that far. As an explanation it seriously leaks, because paradoxically those destined to reject and be damned are held accountable for rejecting and, even more strikingly, are, it is assumed, invited to respond positively to the gospel and so swap from being damned to being blessed. Mark does not dissolve the tension, but we may assume his rhetoric in this regard leaked as it did with most others.

Mark has Jesus use the rhetoric of divine determination but appears not to have followed it so far as to close the door on mission, including to those who reject. Mark's Jesus reports family division: "Brother will betray brother to death and fathers, sons, and children will turn against their parents and have them killed. 13 And you will be hated by everyone for my sake" (13:12–13).* Mark had reported the rejection Jesus found in his own family, who feared he had lost his mind, which Mark strikingly juxtaposed to his opponents who say the same using the language of demon possession, and ended by having Jesus conclude that his family now were those who embrace God's will (3:21–35). Some would find comfort in this, but I suspect that for many such division would have been traumatic.

The assumption that informs Mark's declaration that the disaster of 70 CE, which saw the temple's destruction and much slaughter, was an act of God's judgement is similarly a judgement that deserves questioning. It functions in Mark to bring comfort and assurance to his listeners. For some it would have been traumatic; for others, perhaps, at worst a temptation to self-congratulation and smugness.

DEALING WITH REJECTION IN MATTHEW

As noted above, Matthew takes up the seed parables from Mark 4, but alters Mark's rather stark statement that parables served to ensure that outsiders not get the message. Instead, he brings the citation of Isaiah 6:9–10 in fuller form, as often he does with Mark's biblical allusions, but introduces it not with "in order that" but with "because." The outsiders do not respond because they hear but don't hear and see but don't really see. "The reason I speak to them in parables is because 'seeing they do not perceive, and hearing they do not listen, nor do they understand'" (13:13).*

Matthew also employs Mark's strategy of offering reassurance by pointing to divine confirmation. Not only does he repeat Mark's story of the divine voice at Jesus' baptism (now declared to all, not just Jesus) (3:17) and at his transfiguration (17:5), but he also prefaces his story with the story of the divine miracle of Jesus' conception, and bookends it with reports of heavenly interventions and earthquakes.

Matthew's birth narratives also echo stories of old, such as when Joseph and Mary are confronted by a murderous king Herod, who like Pharaoh is bent on killing infants, and flee to Egypt and then have their own exodus. Matthew weaves an allusion also to another king who threatened Israel on its journey from Egypt, namely King Barak of Moab. He commissioned his prophet, Balaam, to curse the Israelites, but instead, Balaam declared: "a star shall come out of Jacob, and a scepter shall rise out of Israel" (Num 24:17), seen later as a prediction of the Messiah to come, and reflected as such in Matthew's story, inspiring the image of the star over Bethlehem.

These, in part, reassuring instances confirming continuity with God's action in the past sit alongside Matthew's initiative of turning allusions to Old Testament texts into direct quotations, often introduced by the words, "This is to fulfil what was spoken by the prophet, saying . . ." Matthew, too, uses miracle stories to enhance assurance that to follow Jesus was indeed to be in tune with God's action in the past and the present.

Matthew shaped his account of John the Baptist, so that he now introduces Jesus primarily as the judge to come, a key role in Matthew's presentation of Jesus. It informs his portrait of Jesus as the one who truly fulfills and upholds the Law. This is in part a response to those who reject the gospel, whom Matthew depicts above all as failing to heed the commandments. In this way Matthew is telling his listeners that those Jews who reject them, often their fellow Jews, do so because they do not uphold God's Law. They are not good Jews! Matthew champions Jesus as the advocate for obedience to God's commands and so frames Jesus' conflicts with his critics in those terms.

This is most dramatically so in Matthew 23, where he has Jesus pronounce woes on the scribes and Pharisees for their hypocrisy and their failure to heed what God through Moses commanded. It was after all what they had responsibility to declare as those who sat on Moses' seat, as 23:2 highlights. In this way Matthew is addressing the resurgent Judaism of his own time, with whom he and his listeners were in conflict.

Like Mark, Matthew depicts the destruction of the temple, probably back some fifteen years before he was writing, as God's judgement on Jerusalem's people for rejecting Jesus' message. He supplements Mark's story of Jesus' trial before Pilate with an exchange between Pilate and the people where they declare: "His blood be upon us and our children" (27:25). He had earlier adapted the parable of the great feast to make it the parable of a king's wedding feast, whose agents offering invitation had been not only refused but killed, in response to which the king sacked their city (22:1–14).

Where Mark uses the parable of the vineyard to depict the story of rejection, including finally the rejection of Jesus, portrayed as the owner's son, Matthew precedes it with another parable depicting the rejection of John the Baptist (21:28–32) and follows it by his reworked version of the parable of the great feast (22:1–14), now reconfigured to be the wedding feast of a king's son, a clear reference to Jesus. Here, then, the focus is the rejection of the messengers who bring the good news of Jesus. The king then destroys the city of those who refused the invitation. Accordingly, Matthew portrays the disaster of 70 CE, the destruction of the temple, as God's judgement for their rejection of not only of Jesus but, in particular, for their rejection of messengers of the Jesus movement:

> Therefore I send you prophets, sages, and scribes, some of whom you will kill and crucify, and some you will flog in your synagogues and pursue from town to town, 35 so that upon you may come all the righteous blood shed on earth, from the blood of righteous Abel to the blood of Zechariah son of Barachiah, whom you murdered between the sanctuary and the altar. 36 Truly I tell you, all this will come upon this generation. (Matt 23:34–36)

Slaughter of men, women, and children are now viewed as deserved. Did Matthew write this with grief and sadness or with righteous satisfaction?

The words with which Matthew 23 ends have Jesus give voice to the sadness to God:

> Jerusalem, Jerusalem, the city that kills the prophets and stones those who are sent to it! How often have I desired to gather your children together as a hen gathers her brood under her wings, and you were not willing! 38 See, your house is left to you, desolate. (Matt 23:37–38)

Facing Rejection

At the same time, Matthew frequently has Jesus threaten God's eternal punishment, pain, and violence against those who reject the gospel. It forms the climax of all five main speeches into which Matthew has grouped Jesus' teachings. How might such emphases have been heard? The book of Revelation has martyrs cry: "Lord, holy and true, how long will it be before you judge and avenge our blood on the inhabitants of the earth?" (6:10). Cries for vengeance belong to the language of hate.

When Matthew incorporates Mark's report about sending out disciples two by two and merges it with additional material he shares also with Luke, he expands upon the instruction that when rejected they should shake the dust off their feet.

> If anyone will not welcome you or listen to your words, shake off the dust from your feet as you leave that house or town. 15 Truly I tell you, it will be more tolerable for the land of Sodom and Gomorrah on the day of judgement than for that town. (Matt 10:14–15)

He goes on to speak of sending them like sheep among wolves and their fate in being brought before synagogues and civil authorities, more appropriate to Matthew's day. He also highlights family strife, citing Mark's material from Mark 13:12 (Matt 10:21), and brings more on the theme in a tradition found also in Luke.

> Do not think that I have come to bring peace to the earth; I have not come to bring peace, but a sword. 35 For I have come to set a man against his father, and a daughter against her mother, and a daughter-in-law against her mother-in-law; 36 and one's foes will be members of one's own household. 37 Whoever loves father or mother more than me is not worthy of me; and whoever loves son or daughter more than me is not worthy of me; 38 and whoever does not take up the cross and follow me is not worthy of me. (Matt 10:34–38)

Between these two references to family conflict and, surely, pain, he has Jesus bring words of comfort:

Dealing with Rejection

> Do not fear those who kill the body but cannot kill the soul; rather fear him who can destroy both soul and body in hell. 29 Are not two sparrows sold for a penny? Yet not one of them will fall to the ground unperceived by your Father. 30 And even the hairs of your head are all counted. 31 So do not be afraid; you are of more value than many sparrows. (Matt 10:28–31)

This is reassurance in facing the prospect of suffering. Earlier in the Sermon on the Mount we find similar comfort.

> Blessed are those who are persecuted for righteousness' sake, for theirs is the kingdom of heaven. 11 Blessed are you when people revile you and persecute you and utter all kinds of evil against you falsely on my account. 12 Rejoice and be glad, for your reward is great in heaven, for in the same way they persecuted the prophets who were before you. (Matt 5:10–11; similarly, Luke 6:22–23)

In the following chapter, Matthew returns to the theme of judgement on cities that have rejected Jesus' message, as with God's judgement on Sodom.

> Woe to you, Chorazin! Woe to you, Bethsaida! For if the deeds of power done in you had been done in Tyre and Sidon, they would have repented long ago in sackcloth and ashes. 22 But I tell you, on the day of judgement it will be more tolerable for Tyre and Sidon than for you. 23 And you, Capernaum, will you be exalted to heaven? No, you will be brought down to Hades. For if the deeds of power done in you had been done in Sodom, it would have remained until this day. 24 But I tell you that on the day of judgement it will be more tolerable for the land of Sodom than for you. (Matt 11:21–24)

Matthew frequently has Jesus motivate change by referring to the threat of eternal damnation. Focusing on judgement when encountering rejection will for some have been some comfort and perhaps even evoked a sense of justice in the sense of knowing that God will take vengeance on those who reject their message. This

Facing Rejection

is a slippery slope that takes one far from the values of love at the heart of the gospel.

The transition from the hurt and pain of rejection to the language of hate and acts of violence is an all too common human experience. It was inevitable that people would project such notions onto their idea of God. Righteous indignation is then seen to play itself out in an image of God who will inflict pain and suffering on the disobedient. In its extreme form, such thought in effect has God go far beyond what any civilized juridical system would tolerate, far beyond capital punishment, which most on humane grounds have abolished. The image is made as terrifying as possible, with those rejecting the gospel pictured as in a state of being permanently inflicted with pain and violence.

This image of God as intent on doing such violence inevitably makes the notion of God as loving well nigh impossible. At most it produces the image of God as relenting for a time to give people a chance, in that sense acting out of character, or even in character because he finds someone on whom to inflict his punishment, namely his own Son. Jesus then saves us from this God who is terrifyingly violent.

The result is a travesty of the gospel, but it also has wider consequences. Those who have also been hurt and turn to anger can see in their image of God the justification for themselves to exercise violence when they believe they are right. Perversely their faith at worst inspires domestic and other forms of violence. Faith then can justify war and violence against those deemed unworthy. Hate prevails.

The image of God as exercising such violence in Matthew can be ignored but cannot be explained away and creates tension within his story. There seems to be awareness of this tension on Matthew's part because he does much that would undermine its horrible image. Far from encouraging believers to gloat at what has befallen their Jewish brothers and sisters, Matthew adds a twist to his parable of the wedding feast and has one of the believers also consigned to that awful fate, for not coming to the wedding feast

Dealing with Rejection

appropriately clothed, an image for being committed to love as the fulfillment of the Law, being clothed in righteousness.

Similarly, Matthew has Jesus conclude his final discourse with warnings to disciples of his time that what will count at the judgement will not be any status they might claim as they hail him Lord, but whether their lives have shown love and compassion for his own. He has Jesus make a similar challenge in the climax of the Sermon on the Mount (7:21–23). The parables of the girls who run out of oil, or the servant who buried the talent, and the sheep and the goats in Matthew 25 all serve to have Jesus say to disciples of Matthew's day: your fate will be the same as the fate of Jerusalem if you fail to make love in action central.

Already the clear focus on love as the fruit to be shown stands somewhat in tension with the threats of eternal punishment. Amid Matthew's threatening scenes of Jesus, the judge to come, warning of judgement to come, we also find appeals to take a very different stance.

> You have heard that it was said, "You shall love your neighbor and hate your enemy." 44 But I say to you, Love your enemies and pray for those who persecute you, 45 so that you may be children of your Father in heaven; for he makes his sun rise on the evil and on the good, and sends rain on the righteous and on the unrighteous. (Matt 5:43–45)

This, the sixth, coheres also with how Matthew has Jesus begin his exposition of what it truly means to keep the Law. For he expands the first, "You shall not murder" to warnings about harboring anger and hate (5:21–22).

Thus, Matthew presents a paradox in its way of coping with rejection. On the one hand, it reassures its listeners of continuity with the divine and offers the comfort that those who reject them would burn in hell forever, and, on the other, appeals to love, not only for one's own, as in the parable of the sheep and the goats, but also for one's enemies. Both stances have had major impact down through history and made Christian faith a source of health and unhealth for the human community.

Facing Rejection

DEALING WITH REJECTION IN LUKE

Similarly to Mark and Matthew, Luke, also the author of Acts, offers reassurance by emphasizing divine confirmation through heavenly interventions, including visions and miracles, and like Matthew, begins his Gospel with the miraculous conception of Jesus. But Luke's focus differs from Matthew's, instead emphasizing links with David's city, Bethlehem, and its shepherds, and subtly setting Jesus the savior of the world and bringer of peace in contrast to Rome's emperor also hailed as Son of God, bringer of peace, and savior of the world.

In addition, Luke begins his Gospel account with depictions of faithful Jews, models of faith, exercising their devotion in the temple, and does the same in Acts, where the beginning of the church comes about through faithful Jews, followers of Jesus, in the temple.

Luke, therefore, offers reassurance by emphasizing continuity through the faithful. Beyond that, he does so in the way he structures his narrative geographically. The movement begins in Galilee, then moves to Jerusalem, and from there to the world.

In addition, Luke employs typology, depicting the appearances of the risen Jesus as occurring over forty days before his ascension and then locating the giving of the Spirit on the fiftieth day after Jesus' death, the Jewish harvest festival, a symbolic structure that subsequently shaped the church's liturgical year, whereas others locate the gift of the Spirit as given on the day of resurrection, as in John 20:19–23. Even Luke is aware that the appearance to Paul on the road to Damascus must have happened well after the forty days. Forty was a highly symbolic number, recalling the forty years of Israel in the wilderness and also Jesus' forty days of temptation in the wilderness.

Luke does not portray the new movement as abandoning Israel. On the contrary, he wants any who may be disturbed by the resurgent Judaism of his time, as surely some were, to know that it is they, his listeners, who have embraced the good news, who have not abandoned their faith, not abandoned true Israel. Luke's devout Jews, depicted in the opening chapters of his Gospel, are looking for God's kingdom to come and for Luke it will be based in Jerusalem, whose inhabitants will be able to lift their eyes and see Jesus returning to rule as their Messiah (Luke 21:28).

Luke shares with Matthew Jesus' confrontation of the Jewish authorities. In his account of Jesus' words, the prophets, Jesus, himself, and the apostles are emissaries of divine Wisdom.

> Therefore also the Wisdom of God said, "I will send them prophets and apostles, some of whom they will kill and persecute,' 50 so that this generation may be charged with the blood of all the prophets shed since the foundation of the world, 51 from the blood of Abel to the blood of Zechariah, who perished between the altar and the sanctuary. Yes, I tell you, it will be charged against this generation." (Luke 11:49–51)

He, too, brings what is effectively the Wisdom of God's lament at Jerusalem's failure to respond:

> Jerusalem, Jerusalem, the city that kills the prophets and stones those who are sent to it! How often have I desired to gather your children together as a hen gathers her brood under her wings, and you were not willing! 35 See, your house is left to you. And I tell you, you will not see me until the time comes when you say, "Blessed is the one who comes in the name of the Lord." (Luke 13:34–35)

He, too, envisages a future in hell for unbelievers. "There will be weeping and gnashing of teeth when you see Abraham and Isaac and Jacob and all the prophets in the kingdom of God, and you yourselves thrown out" (13:28). He also brings the parable of the rich man and Lazarus, in which he describes the rich man calling out to Abraham: "Father Abraham, have mercy on me, and send Lazarus to dip the tip of his finger in water and cool my tongue; for I am in agony in these flames" (16:24).

As noted in discussing Matthew above, he shares with Matthew common material that has Jesus predict family divisions, pronounce blessed those who will face rejection, portray shaking dust off one's feet as an indication of divine judgement, and affront unresponsive towns with threats of their demise. In general, however, Luke has fewer references to hell and employs it less to help his listeners deal with rejection.

His common material also includes Jesus' instruction, "Love your enemies, do good to those who hate you, bless those who curse you, pray for those who abuse you" (6:27–28). In addition, he has Jesus rebuke his disciples James and John, who want to call down fire from heaven to consume the Samaritans for not welcoming him (9:52–55).

In retelling Mark's account of the parable of the sower, Luke repeats Mark's harsh words, which suggest that parables serve to prevent rather than promote communication and repeats the allusion to Isaiah 6:9–10 in the final chapter of Acts, where we read,

> The Holy Spirit was right in saying to your ancestors through the prophet Isaiah, 26 "Go to this people and say, You will indeed listen, but never understand, and you will indeed look, but never perceive. 27 For this people's heart has grown dull, and their ears are hard of hearing, and they have shut their eyes; so that they might not look with their eyes, and listen with their ears, and understand with their heart and turn—and I would heal them." 28 Let it be known to you then that this salvation of God has been sent to the Gentiles; they will listen. (Acts 28:26–28)

The focus here, however, is not to explain rejection as purposed by God, but to use Isaiah to condemn their rejection and to explain why the mission now turns beyond Israel.

Acts is in many ways a series of stories about rejection, but in each case something positive emerges. Engagement with rejection in Acts will doubtless have been seen as relevant for those experiencing the pain of rejection among Luke's listeners. Mostly, Luke simply details rejection without going further to help his listeners understand why or deal with any sense of loss or self-doubt that they might feel. The primary comfort is in knowing that they can be assured they are on the right path, are the only legitimate successors to Israel's faith, and that now they have a future to bring

Dealing with Rejection

their good news to their world. The only explanation offered at any length is Stephen's speech, which points to the corrupt temple leadership and warranting God's judgement.

> You stiff-necked people, uncircumcised in heart and ears, you are for ever opposing the Holy Spirit, just as your ancestors used to do. 52 Which of the prophets did your ancestors not persecute? They killed those who foretold the coming of the Righteous One, and now you have become his betrayers and murderers. 53 You are the ones that received the law as ordained by angels, and yet you have not kept it. (Acts 7:51–53)

Solidarity with the prophets informs not only their understanding of the rejection of Jesus but also the rejection that they face, as Luke's version of a saying, elsewhere focused on acceptance, states: "Whoever listens to you listens to me, and whoever rejects you rejects me, and whoever rejects me rejects the one who sent me" (Luke 10:16; contrast Matt 10:40). That solidarity is also present in the beatitude:

> Blessed are you when people hate you, and when they exclude you, revile you, and defame you on account of the Son of Man. 23 Rejoice on that day and leap for joy, for surely your reward is great in heaven; for that is what their ancestors did to the prophets. (Luke 6:22–23)

One of the striking strategies for dealing with rejection was to make the claim that they, the true believers, alone had access to salvation, because, as Luke has Peter put it,

> This Jesus is "the stone that was rejected by you, the builders; it has become the cornerstone." 12 There is salvation in no one else, for there is no other name under heaven given among mortals by which we must be saved. (Acts 4:11–12, citing Ps 118:22)

Not unique to Luke, this claim represents a breaking point, a claim to monopoly, and a denial that Jews not joining the movement have salvation. At one level, claiming alone to have the way to salvation, would have made mission easier and clearer. They were offering something that no one else could offer. In Jesus they had exclusive access to salvation. All others were disenfranchised as bearers of salvation. Luke claims a monopoly.

DEALING WITH REJECTION IN JOHN

The Fourth Gospel is inspired in part by the myth of Wisdom, which Jewish literature from Proverbs 8 onwards, through Ben Sira, the Wisdom of Solomon and 1 Enoch 42, depicted as God's companion and agent both in creation and in engaging with Israel. John 1, which uses this tradition and speaks of the Word rather than Wisdom, is closest to 1 Enoch 42 in depicting Wisdom as encountering rejection. Thus John 1 reports that as the Word Jesus came to his own and they rejected him. Some however did not and became God's children.

> He came to what was his own, and his own people did not accept him. 12 But to all who received him, who believed in his name, he gave power to become children of God, 13 who were born, not of blood or of the will of the flesh or of the will of man, but of God. (John 1:11–13)

The theme of rejection runs through John's Gospel alongside the major assertions about who Jesus was and what he offered. What we noted in Luke about the monopoly claim is very clearly central in the Fourth Gospel. Whereas Mark portrays John the Baptist as offering God's forgiveness to all who allow themselves to be immersed in God's cleansing love, represented in his baptism, the author of the Fourth Gospel reduces John the Baptist's role to that of being a witness, pointing to Jesus, who alone as lamb of God can take away sin (1:29). Earlier the author makes John's role clear.

> There was a man sent from God, whose name was John. 7 He came as a witness to testify to the light, so that all might believe through him. 8 He himself was not the light, but he came to testify to the light. (John 1:7–8)

The monopolistic claim is already present in the claim in 1:12, cited above, that only by receiving the Word can one become a

Dealing with Rejection

child of God, a claim echoed in the famous retort to Nicodemus, that no one can see God's kingdom without being born again.

> Very truly, I tell you, no one can see the kingdom of God without being born from above . . .
> Very truly, I tell you, no one can enter the kingdom of God without being born of water and Spirit. (John 3:3, 5)

The exclusive claim is unambiguous in another famous text in which John has Jesus assert, "I am the way and the truth and the life; no one comes to the Father except through me" (14:6). The many "I am" sayings are similarly making an exclusive claim. He alone is the bread, the light of the world, the resurrection and the life, the giver of living water. Often the adjective "true" underlines the claim and implies all other claims are false.

John makes a number of references to divine determination. John 6 repeats the assertion that no one can come to Jesus unless drawn by the Father.

> No one can come to me unless drawn by the Father who sent me; and I will raise that person up on the last day. 45 It is written in the prophets, "And they shall all be taught by God." Everyone who has heard and learned from the Father comes to me. (John 6:44–45)

These are the ones John describes as "given" by the Father to Jesus (6:39), a term repeated in Jesus' final prayer.

> I have made your name known to those whom you gave me from the world. They were yours, and you gave them to me, and they have kept your word. (John 17:6)

References to those, in that sense, "given" by God to Jesus occur throughout the prayer (17:6, 9, 11, 12, 24). For those among John's listeners troubled by rejection, such claims might offer comfort.

The Fourth Gospel also employs the text from Isaiah 6:10, which Mark used in his parable chapter (4:12) about people caused not to hear and see. It does so in 12:39–41, even going on to suggest that Isaiah foresaw Jesus' glory and spoke of the rejection he would face as determined by God.

Facing Rejection

John 8 goes even further in having Jesus declare that those who reject him are not children of Abraham but children of the devil.

> Jesus said to them, "If God were your Father, you would love me, for I came from God and now I am here. I did not come on my own, but he sent me. 43 Why do you not understand what I say? It is because you cannot accept my word. 44 You are from your father the devil, and you choose to do your father's desires. He was a murderer from the beginning and does not stand in the truth, because there is no truth in him. When he lies, he speaks according to his own nature, for he is a liar and the father of lies." (John 8:42–44)

Here dissent is treated aggressively and turned to assertions of enmity and evil, with awful consequences once the narrative leaves its largely inner-Jewish context and becomes a voice for antisemitism.

In John 3:19–21 the author takes these claims further.

> And this is the judgement, that the light has come into the world, and people loved darkness rather than light because their deeds were evil. 20 For all who do evil hate the light and do not come to the light, so that their deeds may not be exposed. 21 But those who do what is true come to the light, so that it may be clearly seen that their deeds have been done in God. (John 3:19–21)

This asserts that those who walk in the light come to the light and those who do not are people who walk in darkness. They are not people who walk in darkness because they do not come to the light, but rather they do not come to the light because they are people who walk in darkness. They are bad people to start with. They reject "us" because they are bad people. If one might find in Matthew the danger of seeking comfort in the thought of opponents suffering the pangs of hell, here the assurance descends to claims that opponents are simply bad people.

Stark as such statements seem, they remain fragile and what seems closed in fact leaks, as we have noted elsewhere. For this same author has Jesus declare on more than one occasion that people can change. The door is not closed. Famously, John 3:16 declares, "For God loved the world so much that sent his only Son that *whoever* believes in him might have eternal life," anyone who believes!

While hurt and anger inspire denigration and some resort to a philosophy that rejection was "meant to be" in the divine plan, the divine initiative which in John drove the incarnation gave voice to love. What appears a closed system and appears to be all predetermined by God in John is also not closed and language of predetermination is never assumed to absolve people of responsibility and blame for rejecting. Such language implying a closed system and divine planning serves a purpose, in part to help believers come to terms with why some reject them and their message, but the author clearly does not apply it strictly and so it should not be taken as absolute. Sadly, its legacy, when not read in the context of its rhetorical function, has fed antisemitism and hate.

Another aspect of helping people come to terms with rejection was the need to reassure that the new path they were on was not an abandonment of Israel's tradition. It clearly still matters to the author of the Fourth Gospel to make links with God's action in the past, but the strategy is one that constructs relationship with the past by speaking of reality at two levels.

At the earthly level is the temple and cult and the Law, affirmed as given by God, but now replaced by a greater gift from God at a different level. Sometimes the contrast is between the flesh and the Spirit, where flesh is used to refer to the physical material world and is not disparaged. As the author puts it in 1:16–17, "We have all received of his fullness, namely one gift in place of another. For the Law was given through Moses; grace and truth came through Jesus Christ."* This is now a new basis for Law, a new commandment (13:34–35), and a new temple, Jesus himself, whom John reports as saying, "Destroy this temple and in three days I will raise it up" (2:19), which the author goes on to clarify as a reference to his resurrection (2:21).

On the basis of this construction, there is continuity in the discontinuity, which the author asserts in part in order to deal with the anxiety some might have felt, that perhaps they had abandoned the faith of their fathers or the faith of Israel with which they claimed continuity and whose legacy they claimed for themselves.

The Fourth Gospel makes exclusive claims but does so with signs of needing to deal with the pain of rejection. It clearly matters to account for such rejection and to reassure the Gospel's listeners that the claims that Jesus is the only way to the Father are legitimate. The author has Jesus, himself, promote these exclusive claims, especially through his assertion to be all that his probably fellow Jews had claimed of Torah as God's Wisdom. It portrays Jesus, now, as God's Wisdom, God's Word.

At the same time as reasserting these claims and so reassuring its listeners, the Fourth Gospel engages in the issues of the rejection of such claims. Wild generalizations that assert that their rejection was predetermined by God or that they are bad people and therefore were not open to the gospel serve also to reassure its listeners that their choice to believe was not an aberration but a work of God. They were chosen. Those rejecting were not. Yet alongside these extreme and dangerous generalizations the author continues to assert the possibility of change, that those who reject might turn and be born again.

The Fourth Gospel's depiction of Jesus' final words to his disciples in John 13—17 puts great emphasis on unity and love among the disciples, very likely because the author saw such unity threatened in his time. First John, composed probably not long afterwards by someone from the same circle, reports such a division and seeks to help people cope with the hurt and anger that such division will have caused by asserting that such rejecting people never really belonged, a variant version of the questionable strategy of explaining rejection as foreordained:

> They went out from us, but they did not belong to us; for if they had belonged to us, they would have remained with us. But by going out they made it plain that none of them belongs to us. (1 John 2:19)

DEALING WITH REJECTION

As we have seen, part of helping the listeners come to terms with what seems to have been a memory of pain at such rejection and separation was the author of John's Gospel's construction of a continuity based on a dualism. It affirmed the former and earthly cult as God's gift but identified it as a mere reflection and so foreshadowing of what has now come as the greater gift at the level of the Spirit. This was an assurance based on a claim of continuity amid a clear sense of the pain and problem of obvious discontinuity.

DEALING WITH REJECTION IN HEBREWS

The model of arguing continuity in discontinuity is elaborated more extensively in the Letter to the Hebrews. While nowhere addressing the pain of rejection directly, the author clearly seeks to reassure his listeners in his "word of encouragement" (13:22) that their newfound faith is in continuity with the faith of their fathers. For it begins with reference to God having spoken to (their) fathers through the prophets (1:1). For some, that might have been a literal reference to their Jewish ancestors. For others, it will give expression to their laying claim to Israel's heritage as a matter of identity, whether as prior converts to Judaism, or as non-Jews who had come to embrace the gospel of Jesus, which was steeped in Israel's religious tradition.

The author is clearly intent on assuring his listeners that their newfound faith in Jesus is indeed at one with that tradition. As in John's Gospel, this claim is made by arguing that what has come about in Jesus was intended by God, foretold and prefigured in God's relationship with Israel. The contrast between the old and the new has two dimensions: time and space. Thus, the opening sentence of the letter highlights God as having spoken "in these last days through a Son," but also contrasts different modes of God's speaking: "in many and various ways" and now simply "through a Son" (1:1).

The "many and various ways" signals something much more extensive, namely that the institutions of the old foreshadowed what was to come in the new. But even more tellingly, the author uses popular Platonic thinking combined with apocalyptic belief in a heavenly world, to argue that the institutions of the old were earthly reflections of a heavenly reality. Partly inspired by the account in Exodus of Moses seeing the pattern for the earthly tabernacle in the heavenly prototype, the author depicts the worship cult of the old as mere imperfect reflections of the heavenly. The true temple is in heaven. Thus, he writes:

> They offer worship in a sanctuary that is a sketch and shadow of the heavenly one; for Moses, when he was about to erect the tent, was warned, "See that you make everything according to the pattern that was shown you on the mountain." (Heb 8:5, citing Exod 25:40)

He went a good deal further by arguing not only that the earthly is but a reflection of the heavenly, but also that it was, in addition, inadequate to achieve what was needed.

> Since the law has only a shadow of the good things to come and not the true form of these realities, it can never, by the same sacrifices that are continually offered year after year, make perfect those who approach. (Heb 10:1)

Its high priests kept needing to repeat atonement offerings, so that in his strongest statement the author asserts that it was in fact useless for achieving what was needed.

> There is, on the one hand, the abrogation of an earlier commandment because it was weak and useless 19 (for the law made nothing perfect); there is, on the other hand, the introduction of a better hope, through which we approach God. (Heb 7:18–19)*

That achievement has now been met through the action of Jesus as high priest, who offered himself, and then presented the finished work in the true, heavenly holy of holies before God, having permanently dealt with human sin and alienation from God.

> But when Christ came as a high priest of the good things that have come, then through the greater and perfect tent (not made with hands, that is, not of this creation), 12 he

entered once for all into the Holy Place, not with the blood of goats and calves, but with his own blood, having achieved eternal redemption. (Heb 9:11–12)*

As in John, this strategy is designed to meet any anxiety that the faithful might have parted company with the faith of Israel. Far from doing so, they have embraced what God foretold and foreshadowed through Israel's cult. The temporal (promise fulfillment) and spatial (heavenly earthly) dualism was to satisfy such concerns and assure listeners of continuity, despite the obvious discontinuity. Some would have found this helpful. Opponents would have seen it as contrived.

Hebrews also deals with the prospect that some belonging to the community might leave it and so issues the stern warning that for such people there is no way back (6:4–6), a stance which later created enormous problems because it denied the possibility of return, such as we see that grace made possible already for Peter.

DEALING WITH REJECTION IN PAUL

In the letters of Paul, written around three decades earlier than the Gospels, we are dealing with a different kind of literature. Paul is addressing congregations, many of whom had him as their founder. He writes to address local issues, but also makes reference to what was going on more broadly in the Jesus movement of his time.

Whereas Acts mostly portrays Paul in conflict with local Jews in the cities he visited, there are only occasional references in his letters to his experiences of rejection by fellow Jews. It is to be assumed often when he mentions persecution, though that can also come from civil authorities. It is most dramatically represented in his comment in 2 Corinthians: "Five times I have received from the Jews the forty lashes minus one. Three times I was beaten with rods. Once I received a stoning" (11:24–25).

Paul's letters are full of indications that he was in conflict with others, but these others were fellow Jewish members of the Jesus movement. Sometimes he speaks of them in disparaging language such as "false apostles" (2 Cor 11:13) or "dogs": "Beware of the dogs, beware of the evil workers, beware of those who mutilate the flesh!" (Phil 3:2), who were insisting that gentiles be circumcised, or when in Galatians he similarly shows his exasperation with them in the outburst, "I wish those who unsettle you would castrate themselves!" (5:12).

Mostly, however, he engages in argument to counter their claims and demands. This is in contrast to later letters written in Paul's name, which resort to name calling with little or no engagement in argument. A celebrated instance of Paul's engagement in argument is when he reports in Galatians how his companion Barnabas and Peter withdrew from regular table fellowship with gentile believers in Antioch as a result of a delegation from Jesus' brother, James, in Jerusalem (2:11–14). Paul goes into detail to ground his response, arguing that in Christ discrimination against gentiles has no place (2:15—3:29), concluding, "There is no longer Jew or Greek, there is no longer slave or free, there is no longer male and female; for all of you are one in Christ Jesus" (3:28). There should be no barrier to regular table fellowship with all.

His most extensive response to criticism and rejection by fellow Jewish believers is to be found in Romans. In the process he gives us an account of his gospel. At one level it is exclusive in demanding that turning to Christ and believing what his death accomplished, namely reconciliation with God, justification, is the only way to salvation and that a commitment to keep the Law did not suffice because it always led to failure (3:21–26). At another level, it was not totally exclusive because he can then cite Abraham as in right standing with God, that is, having justification, on the basis of his faith (4:1–5), allowing the possibility that others like Abraham with such faith might also have salvation. Against this, however, was the implication that if God had now established a new way for salvation, namely by faith in Jesus and what his death achieved, then anything other than embracing that faith was to reject God's initiative and so reject God.

DEALING WITH REJECTION

Paul faced criticism for his gospel because his fellow Jewish believers saw it as devaluing their common Jewish heritage. In his early chapters Paul has, therefore, to defend himself against that charge and to argue that he does recognize Israel's favored position in being blessed with that heritage (3:1-2). His letter makes the case that his gospel, far from setting people on a course toward self-indulgent lawless freedom (6:1-2), when properly understood, sets them free from guilt and fear and empowers them not only to live up to the standard of the Law but to exceed it (8:1-4).

It is above all in Romans 9—11 that we find Paul grappling with the fact that most of his fellow Jews had not embraced the Jesus movement and the gospel in any form. Here we find not anger and hate but sadness. He begins, "I am speaking the truth in Christ—I am not lying; my conscience confirms it by the Holy Spirit—I have great sorrow and unceasing anguish in my heart" (9:1-2).

We then see Paul rehearse a range of attempts to come to terms with this pain. He begins with the notion that their rejection reflects not a failure on God's part but rather God's intention, appealing to the stories of the patriarchs, in which God chose Isaac not Ishmael, and Jacob rather than Esau, citing Malachi 1:1-2, "I have loved Jacob, but I have hated Esau" (9:13). Sensitive to the shocking nature of this claim, he then defends this understanding of God's actions by declaring that choosing some and rejecting others is God's right.

This then is Paul's version of what we found in Mark's use of Isaiah 6:9-10. God chooses some and rejects others, again citing Scripture in support, "I will have mercy on whom I have mercy, and I will have compassion on whom I have compassion" (Exod 33:19; Rom 9:25). Paul is aware of the objection that this implies that those who reject are not to blame for doing so but fends it off. Like a potter, God can shape events to suit his plans. Paul then softens the harshness of these comments by hinting that God has a purpose in having the Jews reject the gospel, because it has meant that the gospel has now gone also to Gentiles, people not originally God's people, alluding to Hosea 2:1, 25 (9:19-26).

He continues with reference to Isaiah's prophecy that "Though the number of the children of Israel were like the sand of the sea, only a remnant of them will be saved; for the Lord will execute his sentence on the earth quickly and decisively" (Isa 28:22; Rom 9:27–28). Applied to the situation Paul is defending, he thereby acknowledges that only a remnant of Jews have come to faith in Jesus.

Thus far Paul evokes divine will to explain why most Jews have not accepted the gospel, but clearly sets this beside an understanding that makes them responsible for what they have done. He then explains their rejection: "Israel, who did strive for the righteousness that is based on the law, did not succeed in fulfilling that law. Why not? Because they did not strive for it on the basis of faith, but as if it were based on works" (9:31–32).

There is a tension between the claim that God determines who responds and who does not and the claim that people are responsible for whether they respond or not. Alongside this is the assumption that some can change their minds and choose to believe. Paul would have to say that that was also predetermined by God. Clearly, we are not dealing with a kind of determining by God that would remove responsibility from people. They are to blame and will face judgement if they reject the gospel. In that sense there is the kind of leak in the determinism that we find elsewhere when notions of predestination come into play, such as in the Fourth Gospel discussed above.

Paul has not resolved the tension nor has he abandoned compassion for his fellow Jews who reject the gospel and so affirms: "Brothers and sisters, my heart's desire and prayer to God for them is that they may be saved" (10:1). He goes on to expand the summary explanation given just a few verses earlier. Their fault is that they try to establish their own acceptability, rightness, before God by keeping the commandments, even though they do so with zeal for God (10:3), but fail to see that God offers such status, righteousness, as a gift and offers it to all (10:4). Paul goes on to acclaim this generosity of God as the good news, the gospel, offered to all and then to bemoan Israel's failure to accept this offer: "But of Israel he

Dealing with Rejection

says, 'All day long I have held out my hands to a disobedient and contrary people'" (10:21, citing Isa 65:2).

Paul, however, is not finished, his response not settled. His struggle continues. He comes back to the painful question: "I ask, then, has God rejected his people?" (11:1). His response is a resounding: "By no means!" (11:1). He appeals to Elijah's feeling forsaken by all only to be told there were thousands remaining faithful (11:2–4). That only goes so far, and Paul reverts to the notion that some are chosen and some are not when he employs the traditional notion of God hardening some people's minds, thus blocking them from responding. In words reminiscent of Isaiah 6:9–10, he cites a mixture of Deuteronomy 29:3 and Isaiah 29:10, "God gave them a sluggish spirit, eyes that would not see and ears that would not hear, down to this very day" (11:8) and cites Psalm 68:22–23 to similar effect.

This does not yet resolve the issue, so Paul continues: "So I ask, have they stumbled so as to fall?" and again replies: "By no means!" (11:11). It is very clear that Paul is having difficulty contemplating that God would give up on Israel, his fellow Jews. He clearly finds the notion that God would cease loving them very difficult, much as it is the logical consequence of most of what he has said thus far.

His next step makes something good out of their failure to believe, already hinted at in 9:19–26, namely that the result of the Jews' rejection has been the extending of the gospel also to gentiles, which then prompts him to address his gentile listeners, cautioning them not to feel superior. It is in this context that he describes them as grafted into the tree of being God's people, but then goes one step further to make the claim that the branches that had been broken off, namely those who rejected the gospel, are to be grafted back in (11:17–24).

At first, he is referring to those Jews who had rejected the gospel but had then come to believe (11:23). Then, however, he dares to acclaim a mystery that flows from his persistence in believing in God as compassionate, namely, "I want you to understand this mystery: a hardening has come upon part of Israel, until the full number of the Gentiles has come in. And so all Israel will be saved" (11:25–26).

He identifies the reason for his assertion in what follows: "As regards the gospel they are enemies of God for your sake; but as regards election they are beloved, for the sake of their ancestors; for the gifts and the calling of God are irrevocable" (11:28). This is an extraordinary claim. People have tried to work out what Paul would have meant, in particular, how this could come to be. Does he envisage that there will be a successful mission to Jews in the end and that the success of the Gentile mission will be enough to persuade them all to turn to Christ? Or is he thinking of some other means?

What is clear is that Paul cannot contemplate that God would give up on Israel, his beloved, and offers no further explanation of what he calls a "mystery" but instead concludes his comments by praising God's wisdom and goodness. Love does not end.

This is an extraordinary climax to Paul's reflections. While over these three chapters he has used the usual strategies for explaining rejection, such as predestination but nevertheless blame, he finally cannot believe that God will give up on his beloved people. He takes no satisfaction ultimately in simply resigning himself to the notion that their rejection was meant to be and that they are now to be written off or worse, confined to the fires of eternal damnation. His logic of love, confined to his reflection about Israel and fellow Jews, challenges us to think about all people, not just Israel. Anything other than asserting God's eternal love invites the observation that it represents an unhealthy response to rejection.

REFLECTING ON THE RESPONSES

It must have been very hard, embracing what you believed was God's latest initiative in relation to his people, yet finding fellow Jews rejecting what you had done. The same would be true to some extent for people who had converted to Judaism, and perhaps even more disturbing for them, and also would have been hard for

Dealing with Rejection

gentiles who had embraced the gospel message with its implicit claim to be at one with God's actions in the past.

The fact of such rejection receives attention, particularly for the way it affected families. It is also clear that in his parables Jesus reckoned with rejection alongside acceptance and asserted a defiant hope in a grand harvest, which may have seemed daring to some at the time. The traditions preserved give us a picture of Jesus engaging with criticism and rejection in his own distinctive way, now retold and supplemented with further arguments. In a similar way, people of the early generations took up Jesus' parables and drew new insights from them, in part to help them come to terms with their own experiences of rejection, and in the case of the parable of the sower, helping them understand that some who joined subsequently left.

For some people, rejection is untroubling, seen as something to be expected. For others, we might imagine that it could cause them to wonder if their opponents were perhaps right and they had gone down a wrong path. Being able to see what lay behind people's rejection helped reassure those rejected that they were not off track.

A major help for the troubled would have been the reassurance given in the retelling of the story of Jesus, including accounts of heavenly voices and interventions, and evidence of miracles, not least of resurrection. For those troubled over the extent to which their faith was one with the faith of God's people of old, typological correspondence, telling stories that reflected the patterns of ancient stories, and allusion to Scripture and its citation as evidence that in Jesus they were fulfilled would have brought comfort, as they had to other groups such as the sect associated with the Dead Sea Scrolls, which saw key events in its history as foretold by the prophets.

Another major element of assurance was the emerging claim that only they had the way to salvation and forgiveness of sins. The claim to monopoly accounts for the Fourth Gospel's removal from the account of John the Baptist the central element of his ministry, that is, the offer of God's forgiveness of sins to all. Increasingly, the claim was being made that only through Jesus' death had forgiveness and reconciliation with God been made possible. For Hebrews this meant that the saints of old had to wait for this to happen before the way into the heavenly sanctuary was open to them (11:39–40).

Claims to be the only way also made evangelism simpler. It had some apparently unforeseen consequences because it not only disenfranchised John the Baptist, but effectively disenfranchised the earthly Jesus, who had declared God's forgiveness during his ministry, in line with John. It was in fact always the case that Israel's faith affirmed that God forgave sins, as witnessed in the Psalms and elsewhere. Claiming a monopoly, and then doing so based on the cross, thus distorted faith, so that, not surprisingly, it became possible to speak of Jesus' significance only in relation to his death and resurrection, as though he had nothing of importance to offer during his ministry, which in some contexts almost disappears from view, such as in Paul and the creeds.

A much more serious means for coming to terms with rejection was to take up the belief that those who rejected the gospel were meant to do so. God had caused them to do so. That would also have been a relief from any self-doubt. This response comes to expression in Mark's use of Isaiah 6:9–10 but also in Paul's initial reflections in Romans 9—11, and in the Fourth Gospel. They were predestined to reject. Such thinking sometimes went alongside its equivalent: we were predestined to accept; we have been chosen. Such language can occur in the language of love in romantic relationships where one partner will affirm of the other: you were meant for me from the beginning of time. Paul affirms to the Thessalonians, "we know, brothers and sisters beloved by God, that he has chosen you" (1:4; similar 2 Thess 2:13; Eph 1:4–5).

The language of being chosen, elect, destined to respond and belong, does not always sit alongside language that speaks of those who reject as being destined to do so. Pressed to its logical conclusion, it could result in a rigid demarcation that sees some as elect and some not—a closed system. Paul is rightly aware that this would mean that any blame being attached to people for rejecting the gospel is inappropriate, which he seeks to brush aside. The reality is that mostly where we find such language, we do not find the assumption that people bear no guilt. We also tend to find that the system is not a closed one. It is assumed that people can change and turn towards acceptance. Human freedom to decide remains. Indeed, the language of predestination can paradoxically serve to encourage people to change.

How does such deterministic language help people cope with the grief of rejection? It would certainly relieve them somewhat of self-doubt and would help affirm their sense of identity as chosen. Such would be the function of the rhetoric of predestination. Where, however, it was pressed, as sometimes has happened over history, it might lead to conclusions that can only be described as seriously unhealthy, if one's starting point is to affirm the value of all human beings. For it leads the elect to declaring that those not believing the gospel are at worst to be written off and abandoned to a fate of eternal affliction.

To embrace the notion that some will be thus destined to eternal pain and torment and see this as both their own doing and God's doing, is to step far away from those streams of the tradition that affirm love and the value of all human beings. Some will contemplate their plight with great grief and this will fire their evangelism to help rescue others from this fate. Others will sadly take comfort in this final solution that sees some people damned forever, like the souls of the martyrs in Revelation calling out for God's vengeance.

Those who embrace the belief that in effect God will cease to love those who reject, can then embrace the notion that it is okay not to love, but to write people off and consign them to eternal pain. Such people can then easily draw similar conclusions in their daily life. If it is all right for God to engage in violence against enemies in the future, it is acceptable for us to do so now. It is just a matter of timing. Sometimes contexts where such faith is affirmed exhibit domestic violence, which flows from the belief that in the end this is how God is.

Facing Rejection

Such understandings of God then produce perverse understandings of the gospel that see Jesus as saving us from God or satisfying God's wrath, paying the penalty for sinners, persuading God to make an exception and offer love and forgiveness, or having God undertake this initiative to exact punishment on Jesus on our behalf. Such a divine initiative is then seen by implication as a temporary act of love and therefore to be appreciated because it was an exception to the way God allegedly normally is.

Coming to terms with rejection by what is effectively hate is far from the love and respect we might want to embrace as the heart of the gospel. It would also have no place in human justice systems. Unfortunately, some New Testament writings include statements that stand in tension with the gospel of love and justice or can be read in this way. Such are the statements that imply that people who reject the gospel are not just bad because they reject but reject because they are bad. The anger at rejection reflected in the Fourth Gospel has Jesus speak in these terms and declare opponents children of the devil, declarations with painful consequences when taken out of the rhetorical intensity of inner-Jewish conflict.

The most striking response to rejection that stands in contrast to the anger and sometimes vengeful reactions we have noted is that of Paul, who stays with the sadness of rejection, grapples with it using the common leaking rationales of his day about divine determinism, only to conclude that at least in relation to Israel, God could not ever stop loving them and that though Paul had no idea how—a mystery—love would prevail in the end and they would not be abandoned. There seems no sound reason not to extend this theological response beyond Israel and to rest on faith that God's love confronts and embraces all peoples, not just Israel.

On that basis we find no justification for denigrating dissent, taking comfort in claims to exclusive access to the way to salvation and thus disenfranchising others including even Jesus himself, choosing hateful responses as a way of dealing with the pain and anger of rejection, and writing off dissenters as inherently bad or divinely destined to be rejected and damned to hell. Christian

Dealing with Rejection

faith has inspired both love and hate, health and harm, and those bearing its tradition need to take seriously how they channel its potential power for good in our world.

2

Coping with the Rejection of Jesus

I sometimes wonder when it was that the first Christians made crosses and used them as a focal point in their gatherings. I wonder even more what an outsider might have thought seeing such a cross or at a much earlier stage hearing that the cross was central to their thought. "How absurd!," I would imagine that outsider might think. "How embarrassing! The one you claim as your hero was crucified. The shame! A common criminal's death! What's going on with you people?"

The reaction would have been very understandable. The whole idea of crucifying people was to frighten people, to scare them off from ever contemplating acting against the law. The mangled body and often the sight of birds pecking away at faces and dogs pulling flesh from limbs would have been horrific.

The first believers claimed that God had vindicated Jesus, raised him from the dead, but that wouldn't have silenced their sensitivity to this awful event. How could it have happened? Why did it happen to him? They often had to cope with rejection, when people rejected them; but they also needed to come to terms with the rejection of Jesus and that was then much more than the cruelty of the crucifixion itself. It was also about the fact that their Jesus met with rejection many times.

COPING WITH THE REJECTION OF JESUS

In this chapter we explore how the earliest Christians came to terms with the rejection of Jesus, from seeing it as a disaster, a symbol of defeat and death, to seeing it as a source of life and hope, and the rich and diverse responses along the way as they grappled with trying to make sense of it.

THE CONTEXT OF JESUS' REJECTION

To understand the background of Jesus' rejection we have to go back over a thousand years to the time when the semi-nomadic tribes who would form the loose confederation that became Israel came to settle in Palestine, the land of the Canaanites. The resultant tension between the local inhabitants and those settling mainly in the hill country has simmered for at least three millennia and still casts its shadow over us today. There have been moments of peaceful coexistence, such as those celebrated in the tale of Ruth, and moments of conflict and war, such as is present as I write this chapter.

Israel's early history is a story of such tension and of successes and failures in living with its neighbors. Its relative autonomy in early centuries and under its first kings, especially David and Solomon, fractured when the tribes divided into "Israel" in the north and "Judah" in the south and began to collapse with the rise of Middle Eastern empires. First the Assyrians in the eighth century and then the Babylonians in the sixth and then the Persians, turned its survivors into a subject state, which it remained then as the Persian Empire gave way to Alexander the Great's empire and its fractured continuance under his generals, resulting in Israel being first under the Ptolemies of Egypt and then from the beginning of the second century BCE under the Seleucids of Syria.

Destruction of the temple in 586 BCE and deportation of large numbers of the population to Babylonia was a terrible humiliation. Their return, half a century later, when the Persians took power, also included a new tolerance that enabled them to rebuild the temple in 516 BCE. But the humiliation of being a subject people remained and many longed for liberation and a return

Facing Rejection

to the days of David, with a God-sent anointed ruler like him, a Messiah, the anglicized Hebrew word meaning "Anointed," and coming through to us in its Anglicized Greek form as the "Christ."

The combination of pressure on the Seleucid kingdom in the early second century BCE, both on its eastern front and from an emerging Rome in the west, made it possible for the small Jewish subject state to revolt under the leadership of the Maccabees, the house of Hasmon, 167–164 BCE, which resulted in a hundred years of fragile autonomy under the Hasmonean dynasty. Some idealized the success. Others charged the new leadership with corruption. Divisions were rife. This was far from a return of their idealized image of David's reign. The Hasmoneans managed to consolidate territory and control not only Jerusalem and Judea, but to extend their reach to the northern regions, such as Galilee, where many from the south then settled, including Jesus' family.

The relative autonomy was not to last. In part, internal instability and in part the expansion of Rome's empire under general Pompey, brought Israel back into submission to an empire. They were now on the eastern flank, vulnerable to Parthian invasion, such as occurred in the 50s BCE, and other potential instabilities, so needing to be held in firm control. Rome engaged local nobility to enforce its rule and so came about the significance of Herod the Great and his family from Idumea, formerly Edom, incorporated into the Jewish state. He had successfully beaten down revolts in the north and was commissioned by Rome to rule on its behalf, which he did from 37 to 4 BCE.

Among Herod's notable achievements were building projects, especially his rebuilding of Jerusalem's temple on a massive platform still surviving today. One suspects that this might in part have been an aspect of a plan to ingratiate himself with the people. Indeed, those who hoped for a king like David also expected the king to restore the temple. If so, we have no evidence that Herod claimed such messianic status. Rather, many continued to yearn for a restored Israel and now liberation from Rome's rule.

It was in the latter years of Herod's rule, probably 4 BCE, that Jesus was born into a Jewish family from Judea who had settled in Galilee, in a town called Nazareth. Just across the valley was the town of Sepphoris, which had become a significant outpost of Roman rule under Herod. On Herod's death it was captured by revolutionaries in a revolt against Roman rule, but the success was short lived and then the city was all but destroyed.

Rome broke up Herod's territory, but still commissioned some of his sons to rule on its behalf. So Rome appointed Herod Antipas over Perea and the northern region, including Galilee, Philip over the north eastern areas, and Archelaus over the southern areas—Judea, Samaria, and Idumea—though after ten years he was deposed for cruelty and Rome appointed their own prefect or procurator.

What was going on? Where was God in all of this? What hope was there for change in face of Rome's might? What would Jesus' family have thought as they looked across at the smoldering ruins of Sepphoris? Would they have sympathized with the revolutionaries? We have no idea. We do, however, know that faith in God remained very alive. There were people who still held onto hope.

We are fortunate that the writings of the Jewish historian, Josephus, have survived. He provides an account of Israel's turbulent history. He, himself, had led a revolutionary troop in Galilee in the major revolt against Rome, 66–70 CE, and had been captured in its early years and held as prisoner but was also taken on as a useful resource for the Romans. It helped him survive and finally Josephus spent his latter years in Rome, where he sought to give a positive account of his people.

Josephus provides us with valuable information about movements for hope and change in Israel. He includes John the Baptist and Jesus among their leaders. There was considerable diversity among such groups embracing the hope for change. If we seek to enter their mindset, we can understand that for some they looked to God's intervention by whatever means. That might have come from an otherwise sense of hopelessness about anything human beings could do, given the overwhelming might of Rome. Supernatural intervention was the only way, whether through angelic intervention or miraculous divine intervention.

Facing Rejection

Some naturally believed that one could hope for such help only if one was prepared to give oneself to thorough and careful observance of God's commandments—all of them. Among those following this logic there were divisions on how some commandments should be understood, some sufficient to warrant forming separate movements that we might describe as sects, but always with a view to welfare of the nation as a whole. Such were the Pharisees and the Essenes, the latter of whose writings were fortunately preserved until our own day, having been hidden from the Romans in caves by the Dead Sea during the 66–70 CE revolt.

For others, but also for some among the Pharisees and Essenes, such devotion and hope could also envisage human cooperation by way of revolutionary activity. That might take the form of undertaking armed raids on military units and similar such guerilla tactics. The accounts of Jesus' last days incidentally mention such activists, like the two crucified along with Jesus and the figure, Barabbas, who apparently had led some revolutionary activity.

JOHN THE BAPTIST AND JESUS

Among the nonmilitant responses Josephus lists John the Baptist and Jesus. John was active in the outback regions and in proximity to the Jordan River, which flows from Lake Galilee in the north to the Dead Sea in the south. Indeed, as Josephus tells us, many of the movements and their charismatic leaders hoping for change located themselves in these isolated parts. There they were safe, but, more importantly, there they could see themselves as repeating the pattern of Israel's ancient journey from Egypt, through the outback, the wilderness, and then into the promised land. They, too, wanted to help reconquer the promised land, either by their own force, or in combination with divine help, to drive out the Romans.

This also made sense of John's location there, even if he did not see the hope to return the land to God's rule as something to be achieved by force. He was in that sense closer to the Essenes and Pharisees in seeing the highest priority as turning in submission to

Coping with the Rejection of Jesus

God, repentance, as it is traditionally termed. John the Baptist saw this as a challenge and invitation to all, to submit to God, seek and receive forgiveness, and commit themselves to obedience.

Belief that God forgives sins was central to Israel's faith and normally it was something associated regularly with ritual acts in the temple, not least the Day of Atonement ritual, and with the sacrificial system. Normally people sought cleansing, whether from the guilt of sin or from what were understood to be the ritual impurities of daily life such as bodily discharges, through washing or immersing themselves.

John's innovation was to challenge people to let themselves be submersed in the Jordan River by himself. Doing it this way symbolized more strongly that it was God who does the cleansing. The novelty resulted in his being given the designation, probably as a nickname, John the immerser, traditionally, John the Baptizer. Priestly circles appear to have viewed this with some unease, because it was normally associated with rituals for which they had responsibility, but there was nothing heretical about it, so their unease never went beyond that.

John's call to all to repent and be immersed as a way of opening themselves to God's forgiveness was not an end in itself. Rather, John portrayed it as preparation for God's coming intervention at last to bring hope to Israel. His initiative of offering baptism for the forgiveness of sins to all is sometimes forgotten when the later Christian movement began to claim that it alone had a monopoly on forgiveness of sins and that this became possible only through the death of Jesus, by which they unwittingly disenfranchised John, but also Israel's faith and Jesus himself who offered God's forgiveness during his ministry.

Where does Jesus fit into the diverse range of movements seeking change? We can only imagine what might have gone through Jesus' mind as he was growing up. We can expect he would have known what happened across the valley in Sepphoris and why. In his youth it was being rebuilt by Herod Antipas. Did he visit it, or did he perhaps work there, as the description of his and his father's occupation as builders might suggest? We can

Facing Rejection

never know. We can consider it very likely that he was familiar with movements of hope of his time.

We are on firm ground in linking him with John the Baptist, because our sources report that he submitted to John's baptism. This is hardly something people wanting to elevate Jesus' significance would invent because it puts him in the junior position. It is highly likely then that Jesus embraced John's message as well. That included both solidarity with the call to all to turn to God and doing so in the light of God's coming reign. Mark's summary of Jesus' message must therefore be accurate at least in substance: "The kingdom of God is at hand. Repent and believe the good news!" (Mark 1:15).

What has that to do with rejection? Rome's authorities would had have no hesitation in calling it out as subversive because it obviously saw God's rule as an alternative to Rome's rule. By embracing such hope Jesus was setting himself up for rejection from Rome's perspective. Might he have countered that his understanding of God's rule was the world of heaven and had nothing to do with Rome's rule on earth? Not at all. In fact, one of the features that distinguished Jesus' approach from John's was that Jesus claimed that God's rule was already starting to break into their reality. That was matched by the fact that instead of staying out in the outback with John, Jesus took to being active in the land, in the populated areas, with his claim.

Mark and the Gospels which followed him, Matthew and Luke, have Jesus commence his activity after John was arrested. John's Gospel suggests that for a time they were both active. We may never know who was right. But one thing is very clear: John was arrested and executed. Mark brings a tale about his fate which may reflect more fantasy than reality, with Antipas's stepdaughter dancing and his promising her half his kingdom and her seeking her mother's wish to have John decapitated (Mark 6:17–29).

Probably John did offend Antipas by his overly strict disapproval of Antipas marrying the divorced wife of his stepbrother, as Mark suggests (Mark 6:18), permissible in most jurisdictions. The broader and more likely rationale, as reflected in Josephus, is that Antipas saw John as calling Roman rule into question by proclaiming an alternative and so fomenting dissent. He had to go. The same would apply to anyone like John, thus including Jesus.

LIBERATING LOVE

Jesus continued John's call for people to turn to God, embrace God's forgiveness, and, as his model prayer taught them, pray, "Your kingdom come!" The frame of reference for his message of liberation was that of his time, namely that evil spirits pervaded the human community. They had been unleashed by the deeds of wayward angels who raped women, who gave birth to giants, who then fought one another to death and from whose corpses these evil spirits emerged. We know this influential story from a document now incorporated in 1 Enoch, a collection of Jewish writings inspired by the figure Enoch, and some going back to the fourth century BCE. An earlier version of this ancient story left traces in Genesis 6.

Sickness was to be explained by such spirits, who like personalized viruses infected people, but nations were also seen to be controlled by such spirits, accounting for their abuses. Hope for God's reign meant hope of liberation, freeing people from the powers that oppressed them within them, personally, and outside of them, so Rome's rule.

Jesus' actions reflect these assumptions and so we see him engaging in exorcism as a means of healing. It is easy to document the way stories of miraculous cures took on a life of their own. We see it in the way that Matthew can change an account where Mark reports that some or many were healed to make it read all were healed (e.g., Mark 1:32–34; compared with Matt 8:16–17). Miraculous healings served propaganda. Even emperors promoted themselves by such means.

Jesus' healings and exorcisms, based on assumptions foreign to us, were not, we can observe, self-promotion, but cited as evidence that God's reign was beginning to take effect. People were being liberated. That liberation went far beyond healing and

Facing Rejection

exorcism. It included the way Jesus by his actions was able to restore people back into a relationship with God and to the community. There are a number of anecdotes that show him engaging with tax collectors and toll collectors, often seen as exploitive and deemed beyond the pale. His version of John's call to all to repent took the form of calling all to belong, to come back to God, who was prepared to welcome and forgive them.

As John's novel offering of God's forgiveness was controversial, so Jesus' apparent acceptance of the unacceptable as people of worth whom God had not ceased to love brought him criticism. Shouldn't he have told them to repent and declare that only then God would love them, not the other way round? His response to the mainly religious critics of his world was to appeal to human experiences, especially by telling stories that stated the obvious if you were prepared to make the connection. So in the parable of the prodigal son (Luke 15:11–32) he said that God was like a father welcoming back a son who had gone abroad and run amuck, even before he knew the son's mind, let alone all he had done. He ran down the road and embraced him. Jesus then takes a dig at his critics when he has the older brother complain.

Much of Jesus' teaching as preserved by the oral traditions and later put into writing by the Gospel writers included such simple parables. Other well-known ones include his parable of the shepherd who cares about a sheep that is lost (Luke 15:3–7) or his parable about giving those who had been employed only for a short time what they needed to live (Matt 20:1–15). His parable of the sower (Mark 4:3–9), as we have seen, was one of his ways of saying that despite rejection and failure, he was confident to carry on just as a farmer sowed seed and expected that despite all the natural setbacks he would reap a harvest.

One of Jesus' favorite images of hope was a great inclusive meal, a feast. It had relevance, of course, for the poor and hungry, but it meant much more than that. It meant inclusion. In parables he represented his ministry as issuing God's invitation to come to the feast (Luke 14:15–24). When we live in contexts where full meals are available to us every day, it is hard to appreciate the importance of such imagery. In their world such full meals were a rarity, something for special occasions like weddings, or shared in association with offering sacrifices in the temple when some of the meat might be consumed by the worshippers, even if the best portions would be preserved for the priests. So the feast was a wonderful image of hope. There is a place for all, just as John the Baptist had called all to be immersed in God's goodness.

"GOOD NEWS FOR THE POOR"

It was one thing to heal individuals of their demons. It was quite another to address the wider issues of the powers that oppressed people. The Gospel writers suggest that Jesus appealed to a passage in the book of Isaiah to explain his calling, where it has a prophet speaking of having received the Spirit to enable him to embark on a mission of setting people free and bringing good news to the poor (Isa 61:1). Luke has Jesus read it as a role description in his home synagogue.

> When he came to Nazareth, where he had been brought up, he went to the synagogue on the sabbath day, as was his custom. He stood up to read, 17 and the scroll of the prophet Isaiah was given to him. He unrolled the scroll and found the place where it was written: 18 "The Spirit of the Lord is upon me, because he has anointed me to bring good news to the poor. He has sent me to proclaim release to the captives and recovery of sight to the blind, to let the oppressed go free, 19 to proclaim the year of the Lord's favor." 20 And he rolled up the scroll, gave it back to the attendant, and sat down. The eyes of all in the synagogue were fixed on him. 21 Then he began to say to them, "Today this scripture has been fulfilled in your hearing." (Luke 4:16–21)

Another passage from Isaiah may explain his use of the term "good news" especially as "good news for the poor."

> How beautiful upon the mountains are the feet of the messenger who announces peace, who brings good

news, who announces salvation, who says to Zion, "Your God reigns." (Isa 52:7)

Originally referring to Israel as a people and its plight of being in subjection, "the poor" in "good news for the poor" could also be applied to people experiencing actual poverty, whether that meant having too little to live on or living with strictures and disabilities. Galilee had its rich folk, especially large landowners, and those close to the Antipas, belonging to the ruling class. But it also had poverty, not necessarily so extreme that people faced famine, but certainly such that it made sense to them to say things can change and to welcome a proclamation of "good news for the poor."

To be sick or to have a disability almost automatically meant that you would be poor, so acts of healing certainly addressed that need in part. The inequality that kept some poor while others were rich was based on how the society worked. Farm laborers would be dependent on their bosses for their life support and those with their own farms and tenant farmers would be beholden to regional landlords. In addition, there were levels of taxation and inevitable exploitation that kept the poor poor.

When Jesus, therefore, proclaimed that change was possible and said things like, "Blessed are you poor, for yours in the kingdom of God" and "Blessed are you who are hungry, for you shall have enough to eat" (Luke 6:20–21), he was addressing realities and raising hopes. To pray "Your kingdom come!" was to express a yearning for change. It was also more than words and hopes. Jesus called some to step outside that economic system, to leave their families and the traps of dependence and risk it with him on the road as itinerants.

Calling some to follow him in this way was already a symbolic protest against the system and an embodiment of hope for something new and different. The itinerants would all be at rock bottom, men, women, formerly rich and poor, and make their way around Galilee proclaiming hope and bringing healing and liberation. It worked because the poverty of communities was not such that some could not put them up for a night and provide them with food. This was a daring endeavor and it succeeded because the conditions made it possible. Jesus did not ask all to hit the road with him, but he did ask all, whether those doing so or those staying home, to follow his message and commitment to be good news for the poor.

JESUS "KING OF THE JEWS"

While we know that some religious teachers accused him of being in league with evil spirits, we have less information about how authorities saw him initially. His alternative movement would have raised eyebrows among those committed to keeping things the way they were, as would his popularity. We cannot be sure whether he claimed special status for himself in terms popular in the day, but he clearly acted with authority. Perhaps, as Mark suggests, he saw himself as one day fulfilling the role attributed in some literature of the time to the Son of Man, as God's agent on judgement day, and claimed that as the basis of his authority to declare God's will and expound the commandments. It is difficult to know what might come from Jesus himself and what might be coloring brought into his picture by those who later tried so hard to explain who he was.

The Son of Man figure was associated in some contexts with the Messiah, a stream of expectation reaching back to the hope of a return to ideal days of King David, a true Son of David, adopted to be God's Son, and rule as his Anointed king, "the Messiah," "the Christ." The problem was that mostly when people looked for the Messiah, they envisaged a military figure who would drive out the Romans.

It is clear that people did identify Jesus as the Christ, the Messiah, which is why the church is called the Christian church, but to do so they had to deal with the repercussions that might flow if it was understood in the usual, military sense. Mark has an episode in which Peter declares that Jesus is the Messiah, only to be told by Jesus with good reason not to blab about it, surely because he knew how dangerous that would be (Mark 8:27–30). You could get yourself crucified if Pilate heard you were aspiring to be a Messiah and we know that is indeed what finally happened.

Facing Rejection

There must have been popular talk about Jesus being the Messiah. Otherwise, it is hard to understand how the accusation stuck and led to his demise at the hands of Pilate. The earliest traditions do not suggest Jesus' emphasis was on his status. Rather it was on the kingdom of God, which, along with many contemporaries, he contemplated was about to come in full in the near future. It is this focus that would have lain behind his final journey to Jerusalem. This was more than the incidental participation in the usual pilgrimage for the Passover along with tens of thousands of others. He had been talking about major change and that had to mean change in financial and political leadership.

The temple was not just the religious center. It was also the bank, the treasury. We know he was critical of the temple leadership. He accused some of deliberate exploitation of widows (Mark 12:38–40). To make his way up to Jerusalem as a person who had gained a reputation for bringing change to individuals and proclaiming hope for change in society was courageous and fraught with danger.

Behind the scenes it is not difficult to imagine that the temple authorities had been aware of his activities as they had been of John the Baptist's. Civil authorities would surely also have been aware that Jesus was attracting a following and his name may well already have been on the books, as it were, of Rome's prefect and his officers in Judea.

To go up to Jerusalem for Passover meant danger and almost certainly Jesus would have known that he would face rejection at the very least. The details of his last days are overlaid with explanations seeking to come to terms with this rejection. Reconstructing what might lie behind the four accounts that we have in the Gospels is an exercise in weighing possibilities and probabilities.

There are clear discrepancies. All agree that he died on a Friday, but Mark and those who followed him, Matthew and Luke, identify that Friday as Passover Day, whereas John's Gospel says Passover was the following day, the Sabbath, the Saturday. Why the discrepancy? Did the former want to depict Jesus' last meal as taking place within a Passover meal context? Or was it John who wanted to depict Jesus as dying at the time when the Passover lambs were slain? We may never know who was right.

We are on firmer ground when we recognize that Jesus' execution was a Roman execution, carried out by Pilate. That makes sense in the broader context of Rome's concern with stability on its vulnerable eastern flank. Josephus provides many accounts of would-be messiahs and others seen as subversives being executed by the Romans. The Gospel accounts also provide such evidence with the two crucified along with Jesus being identified in these terms. Sometimes translated as "thieves," the word used to describe them, also used by Josephus, rather means "revolutionaries" or "bandits." Barabbas, who features, was leader of a revolt. Crucifixions of subversives was not uncommon.

It is fairly clear that Pilate would have placed Jesus in the category of a subversive. Popular movements like his, especially when they promoted change, effectively called Rome's rule into question, as Jesus did by championing the hope of God's reign; they were seen as destabilizing. One can understand that Pilate's main interest would be stability, rather than the fine points of each subversive's ideology. He clearly realized that Jesus was not a militant; otherwise, he would have also rounded up and executed his disciples, too.

The crime for which Jesus was crucified was for claiming to be "the king of the Jews." In other words, he was crucified as another would-be messiah. While early tradition hails him as appointed Messiah at his resurrection (Acts 2:36), it is highly likely that the charge of being a would-be messiah had substance and Pilate dealt with Jesus the way he had dealt with so many others. Whether the charge really was attached to his cross or not, the function of crucifixion was to deter any such madness that set itself up in opposition to Rome's rule. It made sense that Jesus was put into the same general category of insubordination to Rome as those crucified on either side, the two rebels. And it would also have made sense that someone like Barabbas, a rebel leader, might be seen as a potential swap, if that is historical, and not a play on the name, which means "son of the father."

Facing Rejection

ON TRIAL

One can only imagine what it must have been like later for members of the Jesus movement, being out in the Roman Empire and being seen as hailing someone as a hero who had been condemned by Rome to a criminal's death. It would have been more than embarrassing. It would have been dangerous and brought you and your group under the suspicion, too, of being subversive. This would at least be part of the motivation for trying to reframe the event to lessen Pilate's role and lay the blame on others.

Indeed, this is what we see when we compare Mark's account with its rewrite in Matthew and Luke. Matthew has Pilate absolve himself of responsibility by washing his hands and having his wife hear of Jesus' innocence in a dream (Matt 27:19, 24). In contrast he then has the Jerusalem crowd declare their guilt, "His blood be upon us and on our children" (Matt 27:25). This was a terrible implied allegation because it laid blame on them not just for Jesus' death but also for the slaughter of many of Jerusalem's inhabitants when Rome quashed the revolt and destroyed the temple in 70 CE.

Luke has Herod Antipas also interview Jesus and both he and Pilate declare Jesus innocent and seek to have him released (23:1–12). Then Jesus was not legitimately crucified. It was Pilate's failure to be a strong leader for Rome that connived in Jesus' death. In John's Gospel, which turns the hearing before Pilate into a dialogical interchange between Pilate and Jesus, and Pilate and the Jewish leaders (18:28—19:16), the latter are shown as declaring loyalty to the emperor as the only true ruler (19:15), a betrayal of their people and their faith. Such rewriting would later feed the antisemitism that blighted humanity. Already in the time before Jesus, Jews were seen by many as strange and aloof, keeping separate and so inviting suspicion and so pre-Christian antisemitism would marry with such shameful developments.

What then was the role of Jews in the rejection that Jesus faced? Mark tells of a meeting of the Sanhedrin at night reporting Jesus' inquisition from the high priest (14:53–65). Matthew repeats it (26:57–68), but Luke, sensitive to the historical unlikelihood of a night meeting of this kind that would have breached the Law, transfers it to the morning (22:66–71). John has no Jewish trial at all, but just a hearing before the high priest and senior temple officials (18:12–14, 19–24).

In all probability, John's account is more likely. Mark's sounds more like the accusations that in his time would have been brought against church members by synagogue leaders, including that the claim to be the Messiah was blasphemous, a charge that would not have made sense in Jesus' day, but fits more the later times when what came to be believed about Jesus as the Christ did imply a claim to divine attributes.

John's account also has soldiers join the temple police in arresting Jesus in Gethsemane (18:3), a credible combination. The probability is that temple authorities did want at least to stop Jesus' influence and that might well have entailed arrest and perhaps even more. Their concerns and Rome's concerns came from different places, but it is likely both wanted him removed. John's Gospel suggests that they wanted him removed lest Rome use his behavior as a pretext for suppressing them (11:47–53). Better to sacrifice him than to bring down Rome's wrath on themselves and their people. Some of these retellings from later generations reflect less than healthy ways of coming to terms with Jesus' rejection.

JESUS AND THE TEMPLE

The reports suggest that Jesus performed a symbolic act in the temple, typical of such acts by prophets in Israel's history (Mark 11:15–19; Matt 21:12–17; Luke 19:45–48; John 2:13–22). He tipped over the tables of the currency exchange and may have also tried to get rid of the animals being sold in the outer court for sacrifice. This was not an attempt to reform the temple nor just a protest about these activities taking place within the temple bounds instead of outside it. It was also not a showstopping performance worthy of television coverage. Rather it took place in the huge outer court area of the temple, equivalent to around six football fields and at Passover time almost certainly thronging with pilgrims, making it possible for him to do it and then disappear into the crowds before the soldiers watching from the tower overlooking the scene could pounce.

There are variations of what Jesus was alleged to have said. Common to the versions that exist is the declaration that God's judgement would come upon the temple in not too long a time, expressed in the proverbial short time formula, "in three days," applied later to his resurrection (Mark 14:58; Matt 26:61; John 2:19; Acts 6:14). Why attack the temple? It was not the building. It was the abuses that Jesus had highlighted, such as exploitation of widows. Any such attack on the temple would have offended the temple leadership who must have had the event reported to them, but also Rome, which prided itself in being the protector of such sites among the nations it had subjugated.

Another scene common to all four Gospels is Jesus' entry into Jerusalem, fit these days for a television report, as commonly understood, full of drama with Jesus riding on a donkey and crowds hailing him with palm branches (Mark 11: 1–11; Matt 21:1–10; Luke 19:28–39; John 12:12–19). Again, had this been a major event, fit for television, bringing the city to a standstill, we can be assured Jesus would have been arrested there and then. More likely, it was an occasion witnessed by a crowd but just one of many other things happening at the time and not worthy of special attention. Here, too, we find differences among the Gospels, with the first three implying that both the crowds and Jesus' disciples were hailing him as the Messiah, whereas John has the disciples not see significance in it at the time but only after his resurrection, reflecting on its meaning.

> His disciples did not understand these things at first; but when Jesus was glorified, then they remembered that these things had been written of him and had been done to him. (John 12:16)

Coping with the Rejection of Jesus
SEEN THROUGH A BIBLICAL LENS

The image of Jesus lowly riding into Jerusalem on a donkey derived from detail in the book of Zechariah, where the king returning from successfully destroying his enemies returns to the city:

> Rejoice greatly, O daughter Zion! Shout aloud, O daughter Jerusalem! Lo, your king comes to you; triumphant and victorious is he, humble and riding on a donkey, on a colt, the foal of a donkey. (Zech 9:9)

This is but one of many images drawn from Old Testament texts that color the account of Jesus' last days. From Zechariah comes also the reference to the disciples scattering like sheep at Jesus' arrest (14:27; Zech 13:7) and perhaps the allusion to Jesus' blood of the covenant during his last meal (Mark 14:24; Zech 9:11). Matthew's eagerness to have such Scripture fulfilled has Jesus riding on both the donkey and the colt, indicating he rode "on them" (21:7)—hard to imagine! He also drew on Zechariah for detail for his account of Judas' betrayal involving thirty shekels thrown into the treasury (26:15; 27:3-5; Zech 11:12-13).

So one of the ways of coping with the fact of Jesus' rejection was to see it as foreshadowed in Scripture, at least by allusion. It was above all Psalm 22 that provided motifs for telling the story of Jesus' crucifixion. These include:

> My God, my God, why have you forsaken me? (Ps 22:1)

> All who see me mock at me; they make mouths at me, they shake their heads; "Commit your cause to the LORD; let him deliver—let him rescue the one in whom he delights!" (Ps 22:7-8)

> They divide my clothes among themselves, and for my clothing they cast lots. (Ps 22:18)

Did Jesus use the psalm's opening verse to express his pain? Or was this how those who sought to depict the horror of the event imagined he would have done? We may never know. The other motifs are surely drawn from the psalm.

Facing Rejection

What did this mean in terms of coming to terms with Jesus' rejection, his crucifixion? Almost certainly it reflects that one of the ways of doing so was to see Jesus' suffering as the righteous of old had suffered. This was not about prophecy but about precedent. And Psalm 22 lent itself so well to the memory.

It would also have made sense to appeal to the fate of prophets, though this does not feature in the accounts of Jesus' demise. We find it elsewhere. Already in the account of Jesus' reception in his hometown synagogue we find it used, perhaps going back to Jesus himself: "A prophet is not without honor except in his hometown, and among his kin and in his family home" (Mark 6:4).*

Matthew has Jesus appeal to the precedent of Israel's rejection of its prophets when speaking not only of his own fate but also of the fate of the "prophets, sages, and scribes" that he would send (23:30–34; similarly, Luke 11:47–50), and has Jesus declare:

> Jerusalem, Jerusalem, the city that kills the prophets and stones those who are sent to it! How often have I desired to gather your children together as a hen gathers her brood under her wings, and you were not willing! (Matt 23:37; Luke 13:34).

It would have helped people come to terms with Jesus' death to have the story told in a way that emphasized that what was done to him was a gross injustice, especially Pilate's act, but also with alleged collusion by temple leaders. To see such suffering as like that of the righteous of old and of the prophets would also have reinforced the sense that this in no way called Jesus' claims into question, but much more showed him as standing in succession to God's agents.

HIS STORY AND THEIR STORY

Some elements of the story would have had direct personal relevance for congregations listening to it decades later in the context of the Roman Empire. There can be little doubt that Peter, one of the leading disciples, if not the leading one, ended up denying him. He would be the first of many who found themselves exposed to potential danger and saved themselves by distancing from the movement, at least for a short time. One can imagine shame and anger associated with such experiences. Peter's story would make them come alive. His was a rejection of Jesus and those acting similarly in later times would be seen as rejecting the congregation. Then there then might be no way back, as the author of Hebrews threatens when he declares:

> It is impossible to restore again to repentance those who have once been enlightened, and have tasted the heavenly gift, and have shared in the Holy Spirit, 5 and have tasted the goodness of the word of God and the powers of the age to come, 6 and then have fallen away, since on their own they are crucifying again the Son of God and are holding him up to contempt. (Heb 6:4–6)

Others might hold onto Peter's story to the very end and celebrate the grace that did not abandon him but brought about his rehabilitation, even to leadership as witness to Jesus' resurrection.

Some would hear the story of Judas as foreshadowing what they had come to experience, of being reported on to authorities, Jewish or Roman, with terrible consequences. Some would react with sadness at Judas' fate, but others perhaps with a sad satisfaction, such would have been the anger engendered by such events.

The story of Jesus sharing a meal one last time with his disciples would also have made strong connections, including the fact that it took place in the presence of those who failed him. We shall return to Jesus' contribution to the meal, but first we turn to its sequence that even more would have reflected and foreshadowed what many in later generations experienced. Some of Mark's listeners, listening to the Gethsemane story, would have cringed at their own failure to remain awake and faithful in view of the trials they had faced. Others might have identified with Jesus, recalling their own pain and fear as they contemplated Jesus' plight and affirmed their determination to stay the course when it seemed bleak for them.

Facing Rejection

The Letter to the Hebrews evokes Jesus' solidarity with his own in praying for them in their distress, because he faced such distress before them:

> In the days of his flesh, Jesus offered up prayers and supplications, with loud cries and tears, to the one who was able to save him from death, and he was heard because of his reverent submission. 8 Although he was a Son, he learned obedience through what he suffered. (Heb 5:7–8)

Some later manuscripts of Luke's account of Gethsemane include the detail "In his anguish he prayed more earnestly, and his sweat became like great drops of blood falling down on the ground" (22:44), but these are absent in the best manuscripts, so probably reflect a later addition focused on Jesus' distress.

The arrest would have evoked experiences of being arrested or of running for their life in face of danger. In that sense, so much of what Mark and the later Gospels tell us of Jesus' last days and his rejection would have spoken to later generations similarly faced with adversity, and this fact doubtless shaped the tellings and re-tellings. Might some have seen colleagues brought to execution? One legendary account has Peter himself executed upside down on a cross.

Mark's story of Jesus' execution highlights the women who traveled in the itinerant group from Galilee (15:40–41). Mark's women hearers would surely find connection with them, including in the way they stayed close when the men fled. In their own day authorities would discount their significance and place more priority on hunting down the men, but that discrimination paradoxically worked to their advantage, and we may assume that many would have owned a connection with these first female disciples, like Mary Magdalene and the other Marys, not least because in households they had a key role in making meetings of believers possible. They would have held the fort when the men were exposed to suppression. They could see themselves in the story of danger and suffering.

Coping with the Rejection of Jesus
PLAYING DOWN THE SUFFERING

Opposite to such a sense of solidarity were trends to play down the shame of Jesus' suffering, in part to rescue his image as one who remained strong and in control. This was coping with Jesus' rejection by denial. Already John's Gospel, instead of reporting Jesus' Gethsemane cry, rewrites it so that in its version Jesus declares: "Now my soul is troubled. And what should I say—'Father, save me from this hour'? No, it is for this reason that I have come to this hour. Father, glorify your name" (12:27–28).

Luke omits Jesus' utterance on the cross of Psalm 22:1, "My God, my God, why have you forsaken me," and replaces it with the more tranquil prayer: "Father, 'into your hands I commit my spirit,'" citing Psalm 31:5. The account of Jesus' trial in the Fourth Gospel has Jesus engage in confidence and strength, but John still affirms Jesus' suffering humanity. Despite his asserting Jesus' confidence, he allows that he was "troubled" and at his death goes to great lengths to insist that he really was flesh and blood like the rest of us:

> One of the soldiers pierced his side with a spear, and at once blood and water came out. 35 (He who saw this has testified so that you also may believe. His testimony is true, and he knows that he tells the truth.) (John 19:35).

Why such emphasis? Because there are indications that some were dealing with Jesus' death by asserting that he was not exposed to the vulnerability of being flesh and blood but had a body of a different kind. Such views we see challenged in the Fourth Gospel's circles when the author of 1 John makes so much of the fact that Jesus really was human. "What we have heard, what we have seen with our eyes, what we have looked at and touched with our hands" (1:1). The text goes on to declare: "Every spirit that confesses that Jesus Christ has come in the flesh is from God, and every spirit that does not confess Jesus is not from God. And this is the spirit of the antichrist" (4:2–3).

The author of 2 John writes similarly: "Many deceivers have gone out into the world, those who do not confess that Jesus Christ has come in the flesh; any such person is the deceiver and the antichrist!" (2 John 7). These are not unbelievers, but rather are some whose elevated view of Jesus made it difficult for them to see him as really human, let alone as suffering. Later generations, into the second century, developed unhistorical fantasies as they sought to address the problem. They included suggesting that the Christ as Spirit separated from the man Jesus before the crucifixion and hovered above the cross watching on, or that the person crucified was not Jesus but Simon of Cyrene. Such views became popular in some circles and even make an appearance in the Qur'an, which denies that Jesus died on the cross. It reports a claim by Jews to have killed Jesus only to deny it.

> "We killed the Messiah, Jesus, son of Mary, the messenger of Allah." But they neither killed nor crucified him—it was only made to appear so. Even those who argue for this "crucifixion" are in doubt. They have no knowledge whatsoever—only making assumptions. They certainly did not kill him. (4:157)

WHAT WAS JESUS THINKING?

How might Jesus have envisaged his fate as he made his way to Jerusalem? Quite apart from the predictions that Mark brings (8:31; 9:31; 10:33–34), we can be fairly sure that Jesus would have known he was entering dangerous territory. To be proclaiming God's reign as good news in contrast to Rome's was asking for trouble and even to allow speculation that he himself could be hailed Messiah, king of the Jews, was dangerous in the extreme. But he clearly did exercise a leadership role and, however he might have originally expressed it, also saw a leadership role for himself in the future.

Given the political situation of the time, Jesus must have sensed not only danger but also the prospect of death, including a gruesome one. Mark has Jesus three times tell his disciples that as Son of Man he would "must undergo great suffering, and be rejected by the elders, the chief priests, and the scribes, and be killed and after three days rise again" (Mark 8:31; similarly, 9:31; 10:33–34). These belong to Mark's composition in which he contrasts Jesus' determination to stay on the road with the disciples' failure to appreciate his priorities. The three predictions, especially the third, read as a summary of the events that Mark would record in the following chapters.

Having Jesus predict his fate in this way serves to underline Jesus' foreknowledge and status. The present form of the predictions reflects reconstruction based on the values of later generations. Still, the probability that Jesus foresaw his potential fate is high, however he might have formulated it. That could also have included the assertion that he believed that thereby all would not be lost, but that God would vindicate him. Mark's predictions match his narrative. If Jesus asserted hope of vindication, it would most likely also have included vindication by resurrection, perhaps even as part of the climax of history that he might have expected in a very short time, expressed proverbially in the reference to just three days. Resurrection was a standard component of future expectation among many.

ACCORDING TO THE SCRIPTURES

The predictions go beyond imagining how Jesus must have looked realistically at his prospects. For they also include a note of necessity, expressed in the form of: "The Son of Man must . . ." (8:31). The meaning is not that given this dangerous path, he must inevitably expect a terrible fate, but rather: it is necessary in God's plan that this occur. In particular, Mark appears to be implying that this was in some sense predestined to happen to fulfill Scripture. Usually, such implications are indirect in the form of allusions, but in 14:27 the author has Jesus cite Zechariah explicitly in predicting that his disciples would abandon him and in 14:39 declares it fulfilled:

> Jesus said to them, "You will all become deserters; for it is written, 'I will strike the shepherd, and the sheep will be scattered.'" (Mark 14:27, citing Zech 11:7)

Facing Rejection

"Let the scriptures be fulfilled." All of them deserted him and fled. (Mark 14:49–50)

To interpret the rejection of Jesus within the framework of seeing it as predicted in Scripture was another way of coping with the fact. Underlying it is a theological perspective that claims that this was at least foreseen under the guidance and inspiration of God through the prophets. In other Gospels we see this highlighted to a much greater extent. Matthew often turns allusive reference to the Old Testament into direct citations intended to fill this need. Usually introduced with the formulation, "This was to fulfill what was spoken by the prophet . . . ," beginning already with his account of Jesus' miraculous conception, birth, and infancy.

He does so, however, just twice in the story of Jesus' death. In 26:24 he portrays Judas's intention to betray Jesus as fulfillment of Scripture, having Jesus declare: "The Son of Man goes as it is written of him, but woe to that one by whom the Son of Man is betrayed!" Matthew then depicts the proceeds of Judas' betrayal and their use to purchase the "Field of Blood," incorrectly citing Jeremiah, whereas the citation is actually derived from Zechariah:

> Then was fulfilled what had been spoken through the prophet Jeremiah, "And they took the thirty pieces of silver, the price of the one on whom a price had been set, on whom some of the people of Israel had set a price, 10 and they gave them for the potter's field, as the Lord commanded me." (Matt 27:9–10; citing Zech 11:13)

Luke has Jesus give major emphasis to his death as fulfillment of Scripture, explaining to the disciples on the road to Emmaus:

> "Oh, how foolish you are, and how slow of heart to believe all that the prophets have declared! 26 Was it not necessary that the Messiah should suffer these things and then enter into his glory?" 27 Then beginning with Moses and all the prophets, he interpreted to them the things about himself in all the scriptures. (Luke 24:25–27)

And again, when the disciples were together:

> Then he said to them, "These are my words that I spoke to you while I was still with you—that everything written about me in the law of Moses, the prophets, and the psalms must be fulfilled." 45 Then he opened their minds to understand the scriptures, 46 and he said to them, "Thus it is written, that the Messiah is to suffer and to rise from the dead on the third day, 47 and that repentance and forgiveness of sins is to be proclaimed in his name to all nations, beginning from Jerusalem." (Luke 24:44–47)

These instances are directed toward helping the disciples come to terms with his death as having happened in fulfillment of what had been prophesied. Then in Acts, Luke has Peter declare that Jesus' death was "according to the definite plan and foreknowledge of God" (2:23), and has him pray in similar terms:

> It is you who said by the Holy Spirit through our ancestor David, your servant: "Why did the Gentiles rage, and the peoples imagine vain things? 26 The kings of the earth took their stand, and the rulers have gathered together against the Lord and against his Messiah." 27 For in this city, in fact, both Herod and Pontius Pilate, with the Gentiles and the peoples of Israel, gathered together against your holy servant Jesus, whom you anointed, 28 to do whatever your hand and your plan had predestined to take place. (Acts 4:25–28)

In his account of Philip's encounter with the Ethiopian eunuch whom he found reading Isaiah 53, Luke reports:

> Now the passage of the scripture that he was reading was this: "Like a sheep he was led to the slaughter, and like a lamb silent before its shearer, so he does not open his mouth. 33 In his humiliation justice was denied him. Who can describe his generation? For his life is taken away from the earth." (Acts 8:32–33)

Luke then has Philip explain that this referred to Jesus' death, but, interestingly, without any reference to elements in Isaiah 53 that interpret the meaning of his death. It is, indeed, characteristic of Luke to mention Jesus' death, but without further interpretation

Facing Rejection

beyond that it was foretold by the prophets. Thus, Peter's speech in Cornelius's house simply declares: "They put him to death by hanging him on a tree; but God raised him on the third day" (10:39–40). Similarly, he has Paul state:

> Even though they found no cause for a sentence of death, they asked Pilate to have him killed. 29 When they had carried out everything that was written about him, they took him down from the tree and laid him in a tomb. (Acts 13:28–29)

Then in Acts 26, he has Paul declare:

> To this day I have had help from God, and so I stand here, testifying to both small and great, saying nothing but what the prophets and Moses said would take place: 23 that the Messiah must suffer, and that, by being the first to rise from the dead, he would proclaim light both to our people and to the Gentiles. (Acts 26:22–23)

HE DIED FOR US

It is typical of Luke to focus on Jesus' death as a blameworthy killing but also as foretold in prophecy, without adding reflection on any salvific significance it was deemed to have. There are just a few exceptions. In Acts 20 in portraying Paul's advice to elders Luke has him refer to its import:

> Keep watch over yourselves and over all the flock, of which the Holy Spirit has made you overseers, to shepherd the church of God that he obtained with the blood of his own Son. (Acts 20:28)

In one of the two occasions where Mark had Jesus speak of his death in salvific terms, Luke omits such a reference. Thus in what is his version of Jesus' parting words, he has him declare: "I am among you as one who serves" (22:27), which is his rewritten version of what he found in Mark, his source: "For the Son of Man came not to be served but to serve, and to give his life a ransom for many" (Mark 10:45).

The second occasion is where Jesus interprets his impending death during his final meal with his disciples. Mark reports Jesus taking a loaf of bread, blessing it and continuing:

> "Take; this is my body." 23 Then he took a cup, and after giving thanks he gave it to them, and all of them drank from it. 24 He said to them, "This is my blood of the covenant, which is poured out for many." (Mark 14:22–24; similarly, Matt 26:26–28, who adds after "many": "for the forgiveness of sins.")

Luke's version combines what he found in Mark with a version reflected already in Paul's letter to the Corinthians. After reporting Jesus blessing the bread Luke continues:

> "This is my body, which is given for you. Do this in remembrance of me." 20 And he did the same with the cup after supper, saying, "This cup that is poured out for you is the new covenant in my blood." (Luke 22:19–20)

Paul's version reads:

> "This is my body that is for you. Do this in remembrance of me." 25 In the same way he took the cup also, after supper, saying, "This cup is the new covenant in my blood. Do this, as often as you drink it, in remembrance of me." (1 Cor 11:24–25)

Basically, we have two versions of Jesus' last meal, where he gives symbolic significance to bread and wine: Paul's, the earlier (1 Cor 11:23–26), and Mark's (14:22–25). Assuming that they are not based on an imagined account of Jesus' last evening meal with his disciples, they must go back to something significant that Jesus did as he faced his inevitable death. Beside the actions with the bread and the cup, both versions have reference to the future. In Paul it points forward to Jesus' coming again: "As often as you eat this bread and drink the cup, you proclaim the Lord's death until he comes" (1 Cor 11:26). In Mark it reads: "Truly I tell you, I will never again drink of the fruit of the vine until that day when I drink it new in the kingdom of God" (14:25).

While the two may appear to be different, they both relate what Jesus had done to what he envisaged in the near future, namely that breaking in of God's reign in which Jesus would have a key role. It is difficult to reconstruct what might have happened, let alone what might have been in his mind, but it is clear that in offering them bread and wine he was not just acting out in advance the way he often depicted the climax of history, namely celebrating a great feast, but was also interpreting his death as a significant contribution to that event. In his life and now in his impending death he was offering himself for that goal, the fulfillment of hope.

If we ask what he might possibly have meant by such actions, we are helped by the way subsequent generations recalled it and the way such a death had been interpreted within Jewish tradition. Almost certainly it was to see his death as a way of mediating forgiveness of sins. That had been an essential element of John the Baptist's action of calling people to be immersed by him in the Jordan in preparation for the breaking in of God's reign. It continued as an essential element in Jesus' ministry.

Now he interpreted his death as also an act providing forgiveness of sins. His reference to covenant, whether originally as the "new covenant" as in Paul, alluding probably to Jeremiah 31:31, or simply as "covenant" as in Mark's tradition, possibly alluding to Exodus 24:8 or Zechariah 9:11, was language of promise and relationship, the promise of God's reign.

In the story of those who became martyrs during the Maccabean revolt, 167–164 BCE, we find reference to their dying in the confidence of being raised from the dead in vindication by God and as dying for the nation: "We are suffering these things on our own account, because of our sins against our own God" (2 Macc 7:18; similarly, 7:32), understanding their deaths as on behalf of and because of the sins of the people.

> I, like my brothers, give up body and life for the laws of our ancestors, appealing to God to show mercy soon to our nation and by trials and plagues to make you confess

that he alone is God, 38 and through me and my brothers to bring to an end the wrath of the Almighty that has justly fallen on our whole nation. (2 Macc 7:37–38)

We do not see evidence of Jesus putting his death in those terms, as warding off the wrath of God by bearing it himself, but at least the notion that one person's death can have a positive impact for others is present.

We find a similar precedent for representative suffering in Isaiah 53, a favorite text over the centuries that people have read as foretelling what was to happen to Jesus. We have already noted that Luke has the Ethiopian eunuch read from it and Philip apply it to Jesus, but primarily in relation to the suffering. Other elements more relevant to the notion of representative dying or dying on behalf of others come in passages that refer to sin.

> He was wounded for our transgressions, crushed for our iniquities; upon him was the punishment that made us whole, and by his bruises we are healed. 6 All we like sheep have gone astray; we have all turned to our own way, and the Lord has laid on him the iniquity of us all. (Isa 53:5–6)

Originally the figure appears to stand for Israel itself and its sufferings, which it has borne because of the sin of so many of its members. That suffering, again understood as God's punishment, has been taken on board and the outcome is that the tender young plant can now bloom again.

> The righteous one, my servant, shall make many righteous, and he shall bear their iniquities. 12 Therefore I will allot him a portion with the great, and he shall divide the spoil with the strong; because he poured out himself to death, and was numbered with the transgressors; yet he bore the sin of many, and made intercession for the transgressors. (Isa 53:11–12)

It is an enigmatic image that some have speculated might have had an individual in mind. However that may be, it was certainly a rich resource for helping members of the Jesus movement come to terms with his death. Perhaps the reference to "many" in Jesus' reported words in Mark, "poured out for many" (14:24) derives from this passage.

The notion that Jesus' death also dealt with sin, offered forgiveness, however that was understood, must have arisen very early and could already have been something Jesus, himself, intimated. Forgiveness of sins had been a key element of his and John's message. Thus, when Paul summarizes the gospel passed on to him, he affirms this meaning as central.

> For I handed on to you as of first importance what I in turn had received: that Christ died for our sins in accordance with the scriptures. (1 Cor 15:3)

Paul does not say which Scriptures, but an allusion to Isaiah 53 is very likely. To see Jesus' death as not a meaningless defeat but an act which brought benefit would have contributed significantly to the way these first Christ believers came to terms with his death. They could declare: it was "for us." Paul, our earliest witness, provides abundant evidence of this as being very early tradition.

Writing to the Galatians, Paul refers to Jesus as the one "who gave himself for our sins" (1:4), in 2:20 of "the Son of God, who loved me and gave himself for me," and of Christ being cursed on behalf of others, citing Deuteronomy 27:26 ("Cursed is everyone who hangs on a tree") (3:13). In 2 Corinthians Paul appeals to the faith that Christ died for all as motivation to encourage others no longer to live just for themselves (5:14–15) and goes on to declare that "in Christ God was reconciling the world to himself, not counting their trespasses against them, and entrusting the message of reconciliation to us" (5:19). And he concludes that "For our sake he made him to be sin who knew no sin, so that in him we might become the righteousness of God (5:21). In 2 Corinthians 8 Christ's "generous act" of offering himself serves as a model for an appeal to the Corinthians to give generously. Similarly, in Romans Paul urges that believers see themselves as a dead to sin, as Jesus died to sin and lives to God (6:10–11).

Coping with the Rejection of Jesus

It is especially in Romans that we find Paul highlighting Jesus' death as the basis of salvation and reconciliation with God. He was "handed over to death for our trespasses and was raised for our justification" (4:25). In Romans 5 he declares: "For while we were still weak, at the right time Christ died for the ungodly" (5:6) and goes on to assert "God proves his love for us in that while we still were sinners Christ died for us" (5:8), that having been "justified by his blood, will we be saved through him from the wrath of God. 10 For if while we were enemies, we were reconciled to God through the death of his Son" (5:9–10).

Paul goes on to contrast Adam and Jesus:

> For if the many died through the one man's trespass, much more surely have the grace of God and the free gift in the grace of the one man, Jesus Christ, abounded for the many. (Rom 5:15)

> Therefore just as one man's trespass led to condemnation for all, so one man's act of righteousness leads to justification and life for all. 19 For just as by the one man's disobedience the many were made sinners, so by the one man's obedience the many will be made righteous. (Rom 5:18–19)

Paul's interpretation of Jesus' death as bringing about forgiveness of sin is central to his gospel. In 1 Corinthians he acknowledges that to see something positive in the cross, usually a sign of humiliation and shame, is "foolishness to those who are perishing, but to us who are being saved it is the power of God" (1 Cor 1:18). It is crucial therefore to his coming to terms with the issues of continuity with the past of his faith:

> For God has done what the law, weakened by the flesh, could not do: by sending his own Son in the likeness of sinful flesh, and to deal with sin, he condemned sin in the flesh, 4 so that the just requirement of the law might be fulfilled in us, who walk not according to the flesh but according to the Spirit. (Rom 8:3–4)

Facing Rejection

Paul can use a range of imagery to express the significance of Jesus' death. He can speak of "our paschal lamb, Christ," as having been "sacrificed" (1 Cor 5:7), an interesting usage, given that the Passover lambs were not originally sacrifices for sin, though this element is evident in later Jewish tradition. Passover celebrated the event of liberation of ancient Israel from Egypt, sometimes hailed as God's redeeming Israel. Redemption in this sense means liberation, rather than literally a process of payment of a ransom, though that forms part of the imagery. This imagery is reflected in the only other reference to Jesus' death as salvific in Mark besides in Jesus' last meal, namely in his declaration that "the Son of Man came not to be served but to serve, and to give his life a ransom for many" (10:45).

Paul's comment that God "did not withhold his own Son, but gave him up for all of us" (Rom 8:32), may allude to Abraham's willingness to sacrifice his son, Isaac. In Romans 3:25 Paul speaks of God having put Jesus forward as a means of expiation to be appropriated through faith for the forgiveness of sins. This may well allude to Atonement Day ritual, which later the author of Hebrews develops extensively. Starting with the established tradition that saw Jesus' death as the saving event, it adapts the ritual, so that instead of the animals' death being preparatory and the sprinkling of their blood on the mercy seat being the saving act, applied to Jesus the reverse is true. The saving act is his death on the cross and his appearance before God in the holy of holies is the presentation of the finished act.

The letters written in Paul's name continue the focus on Jesus' death as a saving event. Colossians states: "And you who were once estranged and hostile in mind, doing evil deeds, he has now reconciled in his fleshly body through death, so as to present you holy and blameless and irreproachable before him" (1:21–22). It highlights forgiveness of sins: "And when you were dead in trespasses and the uncircumcision of your flesh, God made you alive together with him, when he forgave us all our trespasses, erasing the record that stood against us with its legal demands. He set this aside, nailing it to the cross" (2:13–14).

Coping with the Rejection of Jesus

Ephesians declares: "In him we have redemption through his blood, the forgiveness of our trespasses, according to the riches of his grace that he lavished on us" (1:7–8). "Now in Christ Jesus you who once were far off have been brought near by the blood of Christ" (2:13). In addressing husbands on marriage, it points to Christ's love: "just as Christ loved the church and gave himself up for her..." (5:25).

1 Timothy has Paul declare: "The saying is sure and worthy of full acceptance, that Christ Jesus came into the world to save sinners—of whom I am the foremost" (1:15). It summarizes faith as "There is one God; there is also one mediator between God and humankind, Christ Jesus, himself human, who gave himself a ransom for all" (2:5–6).

Beyond writings linked with Paul we find further allusions to Jesus' saving death, for instance in 1 Peter, which exhorts slaves to put up with abuse, just as Christ suffered.

> He himself bore our sins in his body on the cross, so that, free from sins, we might live for righteousness; by his wounds you have been healed. 25 For you were going astray like sheep, but now you have returned to the shepherd and guardian of your souls. (1 Pet 2:24–25)

In offering comfort to those facing suffering, it points to Christ's suffering: "For Christ also suffered for sins once for all, the righteous for the unrighteous, in order to bring you to God" (3:18).

The focus on Jesus' death as a saving act is also assumed in the book of Revelation. It hails Jesus as "him who loves us and freed us from our sins by his blood" (1:5). Its imagery portrays Jesus as "a Lamb standing as if it had been slaughtered" (5:6), hailed as worthy to unseal the scroll depicting events to come.

> You are worthy to take the scroll and to open its seals, for you were slaughtered and by your blood you ransomed for God saints from every tribe and language and people and nation; 10 you have made them to be a kingdom and priests serving our God, and they will reign on earth. (Rev 5:9–10)

Facing Rejection

ONLY THROUGH THE CROSS?

In such texts Jesus' death was seen as more than the martyrdom that set him in line with the righteous and prophets of old. It was being seen at the same time as a source of blessing. Underlying this was the image of one person bearing the weight of God's wrath on behalf of others, however literally this was taken, and this, in turn, explains language that sees a restored relationship with God, justification, and so freedom from condemnation and punishment at the last judgement, at the core of which is the assertion that it brought about forgiveness of sins. This achieved justification, reconciliation, redemption as liberation, and sanctification, being rendered holy and admissible into God's presence. Sometimes this is simply depicted as the achievement of his blood, meaning thereby his death and inevitably cultic language of sacrifice also served to express this faith.

In Paul it is dominant, to the extent of being the gospel which Paul preached, the cross, and in part it explains why he says so little about Jesus himself. This leaves the impression that by this alone, namely Jesus' death on the cross, was forgiveness possible. There are some indications that this may not be correct, at least in the sense that he could acclaim Abraham as justified by faith—believing God and might have contemplated that also of others, as his discussion in Romans 2:12–16. On the other hand, making Jesus' death the sole basis of salvation would amount to a claim of monopoly excluding all other possibilities. For some, this would be a complete reversal, from the shame of the cross to the pride that through it they now could claim sole access to salvation.

When we turn to the Gospels, it is clear that they did not see it in such exclusive terms. Mark, who knows and affirms faith in Jesus' death as achieving liberation from sins (10:45; 14:24), saw no reason to remove reference to Jesus' authority on earth as Son of Man to forgive sins (2:12) nor to remove reference to John the Baptist's inviting all to a baptism of repentance for the forgiveness of sins.

Coping with the Rejection of Jesus

Some have noted that this specific reference to "for the forgiveness of sins" is absent when Matthew reports John's work and appears as an addition to Jesus' words over the cup at the last meal, so that to "poured out for many" he has added "for the forgiveness of sins." To suggest, however, that this means Matthew denies John's was a baptism for the forgiveness of sins would not make sense of the fact that he still reports that people were baptized, confessing their sins—surely in the belief that they would be forgiven.

The situation is very different however in the Fourth Gospel, where the author deletes all reference to the connection of John's baptism with sins and their forgiveness and instead has him declare of Jesus: "Here is the Lamb of God who takes away the sin of the world!" (1:29). John's role is redefined in that Fourth Gospel to be that of a witness to who Jesus was, parallel to Scripture as serving primarily to bear witness to his coming.

People usually take the reference to Jesus as the lamb of God as an interpretation of his saving death. This may well be so, but is not unambiguously so, because it could refer to what he would do during his ministry, especially because it sits alongside a number of references in the context to Jesus as Messiah and part of the Messiah's role was to remove sin and sinfulness and sometimes the Messiah is pictured as a lamb or a ram.

There can, however, be no doubt that the author does see Jesus' death as a saving event and so stands in the tradition we have identified in Paul and elsewhere of interpreting his death in this way. It may be implied in the famous John 3:16, which perhaps uses the imagery of Abraham and Isaac in speaking of God so loving the world that gave his beloved Son, though that, too, is not entirely clear. It is however present in John 6, where the author has Jesus declare: "the bread that I will give for the life of the world is my flesh" (6:51) and goes on, in alluding to the Eucharist, to speak of people eating his flesh and drinking his blood.

In John 10, the author has Jesus speak of being like a shepherd who lays down his life for this sheep (10;15), and in John 11 of Caiaphas's explanation that it was expedient for Jesus to die rather than to have the Romans bring death on the nation, which

Facing Rejection

the author reinterprets in reference to his death as salvific: "He did not say this on his own, but being high priest that year he prophesied that Jesus was about to die for the nation, and not for the nation only, but to gather into one the dispersed children of God" (11:51–52). John 15 has Jesus declare: "No one has greater love than this, to lay down one's life for one's friends" (15:13). The author can also hail his death as a moment of victorious judgement when the ruler of this world would be exposed and overcome (12:31; 16:11).

At the same time the author portrays Jesus as the source of life and salvation already during his ministry. This is not a kind of claim that the author intends his hearers to reinterpret to mean: he could not offer life and salvation, of course, until after he died, so all such statements about his being the bread, the life and the light during his earthly ministry need a footnote that states "this was only true after his death." That, however, is not the way the author presents it. Rather, he begins with Jesus as the Word who brings life, and so goes on to portray him as offering the water of life, of being the bread of life, the light and life, already during his ministry, through who he was. He offered a relationship of life through himself with God, including by implication forgiveness of sins, already during his ministry.

Like Mark, but in a much more developed way, the writer of the Fourth Gospel can hold together both the traditions about Jesus' death and the message that Jesus in his person offered life and salvation. Unlike Mark, he excludes all other avenues, including John the Baptist, and instead has Jesus declare: "'I am the way, and the truth, and the life. No one comes to the Father except through me" (14:6). This is a clear claim to monopoly, and as we saw in the first chapter of this book, this was significant for the author's dealing with dissent and disbelief among fellow Jews, who are thereby excluded and deemed children of the devil unless they turn to Jesus.

Coping with the Rejection of Jesus

REFLECTING ON THE RESPONSES

The range of responses to the death of Jesus vary. It seems highly likely that he would have known that going to Jerusalem that Passover would be potentially fatal. Even more, he would have seen it as belonging to the complex event of the coming of God's reign, his death like that of martyrs before him serving to bring forgiveness to others. It is also highly likely that he foresaw divine vindication and like the Maccabean martyrs believed that God would raise him up from the dead. In that sense he faced his rejection with hope but without denying its pain.

Mark's narrative has him cry out in the words of Psalm 22, "My God, my God, why have you forsaken me?" One might point to this and claim that he must have given up such hope in despair. Pressing the employment of Psalm 22 in the narrative to reach such a conclusion is probably going too far and failing to see its function in the narrative. The use of the psalmist's language is part of portraying Jesus as suffering like the righteous of old. I think it unlikely that Mark would have believed that Jesus, his hero, was declaring he was forsaken by God and actually was. Yet it would have made sense to imagine him experiencing such feelings and even citing the psalmist's cry. We are left not knowing, but also able to imagine that such a cruel end would have been overwhelming.

The affirmation that God had indeed raised him from the dead would have at least removed any sense that his death was a final defeat and meaningless, for it meant his vindication by God. That did not remove the need, however, to come to terms with it, and certainly we can see that linking it to the fate of prophets and the righteous would have helped.

Very early, however, the interpretation must have also developed that his death, like the death of saints before him, brought benefit to others, in particular creating a surplus of goodness that enabled forgiveness to flow to others. The precedents, such as Isaiah 53 and the accounts of the Maccabean martyrs, spoke of this in terms of the undeserved suffering and death as having taken place on behalf of those who deserved it, so that he died in that sense as

Facing Rejection

a substitute on their behalf. In that sense his death and theirs was like a sacrifice for sins. That gave great significance to his death that turned it from demise and defeat to benefit and blessing.

As we have seen, this became central to the message of the gospel, especially as portrayed by Paul and Pauline writings, almost to the extent of neglecting the significance of Jesus' life before his death. Others combined this understanding of his death with reports of his offering God's forgiveness during his ministry in continuity with John the Baptist, who offered such forgiveness to all, and ultimately in continuity with the faith of Israel, as preserved in the Scriptures that portray God as merciful and compassionate.

Others, however, excluded all other channels to God's forgiveness except through Jesus, including his death, or except through his death, in effect disenfranchising not only Jewish faith, but John the Baptist, and even Jesus himself. As a way of coming to terms with Jesus' death, this was at the same time a way of coming to terms with the rejection of the gospel and of enhancing its impact in mission by claiming a monopoly in relation to forgiveness and salvation. There was no other way, but believing in Jesus, or more narrowly, believing what his death achieved.

Beyond the development of monopolistic claims, there also developed a danger that what was affirmed about Jesus' death could easily become a starting point for trying to explain why it worked. The early statements we have about Christ's death as "for us" or "for sins" are not accompanied by such explanations. In the same way people believed sacrifices work, simply because they did, without theorizing about how they affected God. We do have reference to God's wrath in general terms and it is clear that behind the notion of Jesus' death as bringing forgiveness of sins is an element of his dying on behalf of others who deserved to die whereas he did not.

A literal extrapolation from such statements can lead to outcomes that stand in tension with what we know of Jesus' teaching about God. Such extrapolation might lead to explanations that God was not willing to forgive people's sins, unlike the father in the parable of the prodigal son, unless due punishment had been inflicted, and that therefore Jesus put himself forward as a substitute, taking the punishment, or even that it was God's initiative to free God to be able to love. It assumes that one man's suffering would be enough to make up for what on these terms millions deserved to suffer, at a mathematical level an extraordinary claim.

Such literal extrapolations produce an all-too-human image of God as bound by rules and unable to choose to forgive without the debt being paid. It produces theologies that speak of Jesus paying off the debt to free God. Similarly, the language of redemption and ransom can produce absurd notions that Jesus paid a ransom to God to free sinners or even worse paid a ransom to the devil, and was put up to this by God. At worst, the result is that we have a picture of God quite unlike the God who offers forgiveness, as portrayed by John and Baptist and Jesus, but instead someone who needs persuading to love and forgive, so that Jesus then rescues us from God by his death. Jesus is not like God and God is not like Jesus, the antithesis of the gospel.

On the other hand, it must be acknowledged that the fairly vague language of dying on others' behalf and of sacrifice can lead to such extrapolations. The claims of faith about Jesus' death were ways in part of coming to terms with it, not dogmatic assertions embodying detailed implications. They were the language of faith expressing the experience and appreciation of blessing—closer, in that sense, to the language of love than to the language of logical discourse. In that sense, they are best not treated as premises on which to erect dogmatic structures. They are, then, best seen as ways of coming to terms with Jesus' death and celebrating that through it God's goodness is also revealed, as it was in Jesus' life as he continued John's message of forgiveness, which was deeply rooted in Israel's faith, not as evidence of a prerequisite God demanded to be able to love.

The apparent contradictions that appear when we take religious language literally resolve to a large degree when we take seriously the nature of religious language. It is not mathematically logical. People might well question how a single person's death on a cross at a moment in time could be seen as a substitute punishment for what millions, indeed, billions allegedly deserve and whose punishment would be far more extensive and include ongoing experience of pain and affliction in hell. This is to misread the nature of religious language. Similarly, when people press the imagery and produce an image of God as unwilling and unable to forgive without punishment being exacted, penalties and debts being paid in full, the result is an aberration and far from the image of God given to us by Jesus.

Mark and to some extent John obviously sensed no contradiction in affirming both Jesus' death for sins and Jesus' offer of forgiveness during his ministry. They clearly operated with an understanding of religious language that did not press it literally. These were different ways of saying the same things: that God is forgiving and that in Jesus' life and death we see an expression of God's invitation to a relationship of forgiveness and ongoing partnership. It is, then, more important to look at what language does than to look at what it says. Depictions of the death of Jesus function as ways of conveying the message of the gospel. They are also ways of coming to terms with and making sense of his rejection, his shameful end.

3

Coping with Acceptance, Healthily and Otherwise

"I hate you! I don't want you to love me!"

Strange as it may seem, for some people it is not only rejection that is hard to bear. Being accepted and loved is also hard to bear. If I am to allow myself to be loved and accepted, I need to be prepared to love and accept myself and I may have spent much of my life and energy resisting doing so. For some that will have started at a very early age with a paucity of love and acceptance in the world in which they were growing up.

One of the ways of coping with a lack of self-love and acceptance can be to create a persona that will win acceptance from others on the assumption that if they saw the real me, they would not love me, because that had been my life experience thus far. Some people live their lives constantly focused on holding together their construction designed to help them survive in what they have experienced as an unloving world. The sense of loneliness and fear then generates all kinds of techniques to keep people at a distance and let them near only when they seem willing to take me as I project myself. That can include efforts to succeed in what people will admire, to win and gain accolades, and can be reasonably successful as a strategy as long as health permits. Aging or development of disability or illness would disable the strategy and I might find myself then even more isolated, lonely, and depressed.

"I don't want you to love me" if that means seeing me as I am. The last thing I may want to do is look at myself. I will then resist love and acceptance. If you persist and come too close, I will push you away. That may even turn to hate. Go away!

Does this then play a role with the "good news" of God's love? Indeed, it does. In some sense, the killing of Jesus was a response to the threat that his offer and challenge of love brought. At a personal level, it can be very difficult for someone skilled at winning acceptance for their projected self to turn around and suddenly let such love in.

ACCEPTANCE AND AVOIDANCE

Sometimes the gospel can be construed in a way that enables people paradoxically to keep up the protection of their true self and not open it up. This happens when Jesus' death is seen as achieving a credit or cover, so that faith then means I gain acceptance before God by being covered by Jesus. He created credit that I can use. God will then forgive me on the basis of looking at me and not seeing me as I am but seeing Jesus and what he achieved. I still know that I am not worthy. I still cannot love myself, but Jesus compensated for that by giving me a kind of pass. Transactional understandings of Jesus' death can, though need not, produce that kind of reaction. The logic of that reaction is that God would not love me, but Jesus intervened and covered for me. So, I'm still left with the lonely, unworthy me. Justification is then just as if I'd never sinned, but it is a fraud, because I know I have!

This stands in direct contrast to what we find in Jesus' ministry, where he reached out to people deemed unworthy and treated them as worthy of being loved, declaring by his words and behavior that God cared for and loved them. That never meant God was like a naïve person who could not or would not recognize depravity and guilt. Jesus never gives the impression that God's love is naïve and blind, as if to love meant to pretend, in fact to lie.

On the contrary, Jesus reached out to people who may have made a mess of others' lives and certainly were guilty of making a mess of their own, and refused to write them off. It was one of the reasons why he attracted so much criticism. Why was he keeping company with tax collectors and sinners, a broad category that probably included a range of people from men on the make to women engaged in activities deemed immoral? His response amounted to saying: these people also matter.

His most effective defense was in the form of parables. The parable of the prodigal son (Luke 15:11–32) depicts a father's love for his son, who had run off, abandoning him, and then returns. The father, in turn, runs down the road to embrace him before the father has even heard of what his would have been up to in the far country, not because love would declare all he did was acceptable, but because whatever he had been up to, the father loved him and wanted to celebrate his return. Pointedly, Jesus has the older brother complain, like his critics, who objected to his show of God's generosity.

Jesus appealed to love and proclaimed God as loving. He expressed this also in the parable of the good Samaritan (Luke 10:25–37), again pointedly depicting religious leaders as failing to do so. His parables about the lost sheep and the lost coin (Luke 15:1–10) originally have the same message. God cares, God does not write people off. And we might add: God does not wait to be paid off or appeased before turning to people in love. That is, as we saw in the previous chapter, to misunderstand the way religious language and imagery works. The invitation to the great feast or the wedding feast, as depicted in the parable (Luke 14:15–24; Matt 22:1–14), was offered to all, again pointedly: not just to the so-called righteous but also to those seen as the nobodies and marginalized. "The sick need a doctor, not the well" was his response to criticism for dining at Levi's house (Mark 2:13–17).

Facing Rejection

FINDING AND LOVING ONE'S TRUE SELF

Jesus also challenged the constructions of those who hid themselves behind a façade or who feared to face themselves and so gave their energy to projecting a false self and seeking attention and affection through it. That self was to be denied. That was the challenge. Seeking to save their life, making themselves the center, being preoccupied with construction of a false self was, he charged, to lose one's true self. To find one's true self was to open oneself to being loved, and to open oneself to love, including when it might be costly, because that was the way to life. Mark has Jesus put it starkly:

> If any want to become my followers, let them deny themselves and take up their cross and follow me. 35 For those who want to save their life will lose it, and those who lose their life for my sake, and for the sake of the gospel, will save it. 36 For what will it profit them to gain the whole world and forfeit their life? 37 Indeed, what can they give in return for their life? (Mark 8:34–37)

This is not a plea for people to engage in falsehood, pretending they no longer care about themselves. On the contrary, it is a serious challenge that asks people to look seriously at saving their lives, saving their souls, doing what is best for them, what is in their best interests. Paradoxically, true self-interest is not to construct a false self and hide one's true self, cut off in loneliness and fear, and be busy trying to win affection through one's false self. It is in fact to embrace love and let it open you to being loved deeply, and becoming part of the loving that reaches out to others and also to God.

Mark brings this teaching of Jesus in the context of what he has constructed as a three-part message about what discipleship and truly being human as God intended means. In this he does not isolate what he says about disciples from what he says about Jesus. On the contrary, Jesus is the model. Earlier in Mark 8 he had brought the conversation between Jesus and his disciples where Peter acclaims him the Messiah only to be told by Jesus that his path would be one of suffering, to which Peter objects (8:29–33). Jesus, in turn, confronts him with the words, "Get behind me Satan! You're focusing on human priorities, not God's priorities" (8:33),* suggesting that his response shows him not embracing God's values but human values. That, then, introduces Jesus' statement about losing oneself and finding one's true self.

Jesus' and God's priorities were to follow the path of love, even when it was costly. What Mark depicts as human priorities was to be focused on one's own power and greatness. The obsession with winning, with power over others and garnering adulation, is the false path taken by the self that seeks to construct a loveable persona or at least a winning one. Its origins may be as simple as feeling as a child that one had to compete with siblings because there was not enough love to go around. Such a sense of not being loved for who you are and not being loveable generates alternative strategies to compensate for the loss. The challenge is to open oneself to the love that one has missed rather than to try such strategies.

In the second of the three episodes where Mark brings out this challenge, he again has Jesus speak of the lowly and vulnerable path that lay ahead of him, only then to report that the disciples were in discussion about who among them was the greatest, typical of the preoccupation of people seeking to compensate for their loss and emptiness by gaining power and status over others (9:30–37). Mark then has Jesus place before them a little child not yet caught up in the strategies of competition for love and affection. The disciples are challenged in that sense to go back and start again, to recover their inner child and allow themselves to be open to love and loving. Accept the acceptance, the love!

Mark presses home the point in his third episode, where he has James and John ask Jesus if they can be top dogs, elevated to his left and right side, when he comes in power and glory (10:32–45). In one sense the story is so sad as to be comical, but it reflects the reality of when people strive to compensate for love by seeking power and adulation from others. Mark then has Jesus make a sociological comment: "You know that among the Gentiles those

Facing Rejection

whom they recognize as their rulers lord it over them, and their great ones are tyrants over them" (10:42). It is the same compensatory obsession to establish and flaunt one's value by gaining power over others and demanding their submission and adulation.

Mark has Jesus then return to the connection with which he links these three episodes. Not only is this not to characterize the disciples' approach to life. It is also not Jesus' own way, and not God's, and so Mark has Jesus declare: "For the Son of Man came not to be served but to serve, and to give his life a ransom for many" (10:45). These are his and God's priorities, as he stated back in 8:33. The rest of Mark's story of Jesus underlines this subversion of human norms. Is he a king? Yes, a king enthroned on a cross and crowned with a crown of thorns, a subversive image in the context of Rome's Empire and culture where, especially to be a man, meant strength, might, and impressive power.

The compensatory strategy of seeking power and glory was widespread then and remains widespread. It is almost overpowering and can quickly subvert models that put love not power at the center. Where constructing a self to be loved is the norm, any suggestion of opening one's true self to be loved is hard to take and will find resistance.

Even the image of Jesus can so easily be redrawn to serve its ends. This happens when his resurrection is seen as a reversal, a leaving behind of lowliness, and of Jesus finally gaining what Peter wished for him in the first place. Of course, it is assumed, he wanted everyone to adore him and to have power and glory. His lowly and loving self then became an act, an exception, a kind of interim stunt. Far from embracing human values and not God's values, in this view, Peter was right. These were and are God's and Jesus' values. Jesus' suffering was an interim episode, just something he had to go through to get there. As the popular motto my high school put it: *per angusta ad augusta*, through hardship to glory!

The meaning of resurrection, however, is not God saying, "No, that is not my way," but the opposite: "Yes, that is my way." In raising Jesus from the dead God was vindicating him and his message. Jesus' life of service, and his lowly death on the cross, was not an exception to the way he truly is and wants to be, like all the others who want power and glory. It was how he was and is. Nor was Jesus an exception in the life God, but the way God is.

This, too, has been very difficult to sustain. Many have created God in the image of the most powerful in their community, usually a male wanting power, control, and adulation. The rituals of royal courts shaped Christian liturgies and it was not unreasonable for people to conclude that God's chief interest, like that of the males who dominated them, was to have power and control and be adored for it.

Images of God not as a dominant, self-obsessed father but a mother have helped soften this image, but even more, the recovery of Jesus' message and the rereading of Mark's Gospel has helped us see that God is not the macro model of the person seeking to compensate for lack of self-esteem by embarking on a strategy to win adulation. Rather, God is the caring creator who gave birth to the universe and loves it and us. God does not have a self-esteem problem. God is not obsessed with inner neediness. Alas, such images of God, often, in turn, help reinforce the values they reflect. God then becomes the patron of the powerful and Jesus their chaplain, turning his gospel on its head and the cross then becomes a splendid decoration to be embossed, not a confronting symbol.

It is sometimes not easy to cope with being accepted and loved and people go to great lengths to avoid it and even shape their image of Jesus and God to fit. Such trends are so pervasive that it will always be a challenge for Christian faith to stay in touch with love as the center and not be seduced into saying and doing the opposite. As one deeply committed to faith, I see this as a huge problem that constantly needs to be confronted.

PAUL ON LOSING THE FALSE SELF

Growling at people for embarking on strategies of compensation is of little help. We need to seek to create situations where people will feel safe enough to be in touch with their inner self and allow themselves to begin to feel the love they have lost or never had.

Facing Rejection

One of the most creative and influential early attempts to promote this approach was that of Paul.

Paul's way of talking about the self that one needs to lose is to speak of "the flesh." By that he does not mean our physical body, but our orientation away from God and towards self-indulgence, the compensatory behavior we embark upon when we find being loved too hard to take. In Galatians he lists its characteristic behaviors:

> Now the works of the flesh are obvious: sexual wrongdoing, impurity, licentiousness, 20 idolatry, sorcery, enmities, strife, jealousy, anger, quarrels, dissensions, factions, 21 envy, drunkenness, carousing, and things like these. (Gal 5:19–21)

These focus primarily on antisocial attitudes and behaviors. They are behaviors in which people seek advantage and exploit others in their interests—in part, strategies of compensation arising from felt need. Paul, of course, does not approve. One might then expect that Paul to embark upon a program of telling people what they ought not to do. The Law, which informs his ethics, is very clear about such matters.

Paul, however, does not make that his central focus. Instead, he declares that through Christ's death God offers forgiveness of sins and a restored relationship to all with the openness to accept it. Faith means opening the self to God's goodness, traditionally called righteousness, and thereby entering a right relationship with God, traditionally called justification. This is much more than just forgiveness of sins. It is reconciliation with God, the embracing of God's love and so entering an ongoing relationship with God, which includes taking on board the love for which the sometimes lonely and empty self has yearned and which people can seek to relieve by strategies of developing a false self to win what was lost.

Paul often writes of this ongoing relationship as being open to the Spirit of God. His language varies, sometimes speaking of the Spirit, the Holy Spirit, the Spirit of God, or the Spirit of Christ, but he expounds it as representing a new way of being which is transformative. Thus, having listed "the works of the flesh," as he calls them, Paul goes on identify the fruit of the Spirit: "By contrast, the fruit of the Spirit is love, joy, peace, patience, kindness, generosity, faithfulness, gentleness, and self-control" (5:22–23).

He does not suggest that people restored to a relationship with God ought now to try their best to produce such fruit. On the contrary, he sees these as generated through the new relationship. The imagery is found already in a saying attributed to Jesus. "Every good tree bears good fruit, but the bad tree bears bad fruit. A good tree cannot bear bad fruit, nor can a bad tree bear good fruit" (Matt 7:17–18).

In Romans, Paul is explaining why this works much more effectively than telling people they should be good and keep the commandments.

> For the law of the Spirit of life in Christ Jesus has set you free from the law of sin and of death. 3 For God has done what the law, weakened by the flesh, could not do: by sending his own Son in the likeness of sinful flesh, and to deal with sin, he condemned sin in the flesh, 4 so that the just requirement of the law might be fulfilled in us, who walk not according to the flesh but according to the Spirit. (Rom 8:2–4)

He had just been explaining in Romans 7 how simply telling people to be good does not work, because it does not address their deep inner need, we would say their needy self, and so they find themselves failing and heaping more guilt upon themselves. What makes the difference, what he here calls "the law of the Spirit of life," is the achievement as he puts it of God's sending Jesus. It produced both an offer of forgiveness and an offer of a relationship on the basis of which people are freed from their guilt and inadequacy and so are no longer caught up in the strategies of the flesh, the compensatory behaviors. They are thus free not only to receive love but to share it. Sharing and expressing love becomes the fruit of their relationship and doing so not only meets the requirements of the commandments, but also exceeds them.

Paul goes on to exhort his Roman listeners to let this happen, to let love in and let it do its transforming work.

> For those who live according to the flesh set their minds on the things of the flesh, but those who live according to the Spirit set their minds on the things of the Spirit. 6 To set the mind on the flesh is death, but to set the mind on the Spirit is life and peace. (Rom 8:5–6)

He is not talking about spiritual or abstract ideas. He is talking about the relationship, about keeping oneself open to God's Spirit and God's love and letting the transforming work happen in you. In Galatians 5 he similarly urges people to take this on board and enter fully into this new relationship with God through the Spirit, embracing the love which God gives.

> Live by the Spirit, I say, and do not gratify the desires of the flesh. (Gal 5:16)

> Those who belong to Christ Jesus have crucified the flesh with its passions and desires. 25 If we live by the Spirit, let us also be guided by the Spirit. 26 Let us not become conceited, competing against one another, envying one another. (Gal 5:24–26)

Love produces love. As we take being loved on board and begin to love ourselves, we begin to give up our guilt and fear, and give up our busy strategies through which we seek to compensate for our lack of self-love. That then frees us to open ourselves to others in love. As Paul says, love is then the fruit of opening ourselves to the Spirit who brings God's love to us. The more we become free from our self-preoccupation and the more we dare to open ourselves to ourselves and God's love, the more energy, attention, and life we have to engage in love towards others.

There is an element of spontaneity in this, as there is in fruit being formed on a tree. At the same time, however, Paul is aware that this is not all automatic. We need to engage in the process of allowing ourselves to be relieved of what we may have carried around with us for years and we need to think about how we then direct the freed energy. So, having impressed on his listeners the reason why this works, Paul still sees the need to point out what we need to allow to flow from this inner dynamic. Hence, his comment to the Galatians, cited above: "Let us not become conceited, competing against one another, envying one another" (5:26).

In our day we might need to think about love's application to issues of which the New Testament writers were not aware, such as climate change. Love loves enough to want to be informed, so while we may see what they saw and understood, we have also come to see much more, including environmental issues, climate change, sexism, racism, and age discrimination. We want to love in ways that have an impact and for that we need each other.

Paul is aware of human experience. If you have struggled with self-worth over a long period, this will not suddenly change overnight. Paul sees our relationship with God and our opening ourselves to love as an ongoing process. In Romans 6 he speaks about it as letting the power of love take over and replace the power we might have installed of orienting all our efforts towards self-justification and justification before and approval from others.

He speaks of people being enslaved to the agendas of the false self and its behaviors and then playfully suggests a new kind of slavery: slavery to goodness.

> But thanks be to God that you, having once been slaves of sin, have become obedient from the heart to the form of teaching to which you were entrusted, 18 and that you, having been set free from sin, have become slaves of righteousness. 19 I am speaking in human terms because of your natural limitations. For just as you once presented your members as slaves to impurity and to greater and greater iniquity, so now present your members as slaves to righteousness for sanctification. (Rom 6:17–19)

We are to embark upon a process whereby we become integrated around a single value, love, and doing so are embracing love for God, love for others, and love for ourselves. We need to work at it and the more we do, the more we will bear fruit.

For Paul, the good news is that we can say yes to love and acceptance. We don't need to hold it at bay. We can open ourselves to it and open ourselves to ourselves and learn to love ourselves again and to love others.

Facing Rejection

GIVE ME A PARDON AND LET ME BE!

For some people, the preference is not engagement in a relationship, but just the assurance that they will now look to eternity with a sense of safety. To put it crudely, they will have a ticket to heaven. They have no interest in being engaged in a relationship, particularly not in a partnership of love with God that will involve them in engaging in love with others and the world.

Sometimes, this is the result of transactional understandings of the gospel. I can remember being in circles where the key question was whether one was "saved" or not. "Saved" meant something like saved from going to hell. As a teenage evangelist it was central to missions that I led. For some it meant as little as, "Thanks, Jesus, and now I can get on with my life with little change except to try to get others 'saved' too." Focusing just on forgiveness of sins and not on an ongoing relationship with God, as Paul, especially, expounds it, is one of the causes.

For others, it meant much more than that. Often what people really mean when they use religious language can be much more (or sometimes less!) than what they say. So, for some it really did mean a wonderful incursion of love into their lives as never before and a consequent love and joy that began to transform their lives. For the former, it was little more than another advantage won and perhaps the relief of now belonging to the "saved," a status and a future security.

This was already a problem in the first century and we find it addressed in Matthew's Gospel. To counter it, he frames Jesus as not only coming with the liberating message of love, but also as the one whom God will use to be the judge at the end of time. He retells the story of John the Baptist so that as the one to come, Jesus is hailed as the one who carries the axe ready at the foot of the tree to cut it down or as a farmer before the harvest: "His winnowing-fork is in his hand, and he will clear his threshing-floor and will gather his wheat into the granary; but the chaff he will burn with unquenchable fire" (3:12).

Matthew can then counter any misunderstanding that this was on the brink of happening with recourse to another story in which John's disciples appear to be thinking along such lines and Jesus instead points to what he has been doing in the meantime, namely bringing good news and performing acts of healing (11:2–6). Matthew accordingly portrays Jesus as the judge to come who in the interim fulfills God's commission, which is very much in terms of bringing healing and hope. For Matthew as for Mark, those are God's priorities.

Matthew's innovation in his story of Jesus is to gather sayings of Jesus into five main speeches. Taking up a motif he found in Mark of Jesus going up a mountain with his disciples (3:13), Matthew brings the first of these speeches up a mountain in a way that inevitably recalled Moses' ascent up Mount Sinai to receive the Law (5:1—7:29). Up the mountain in the aptly named "Sermon on the Mount," Jesus does not receive the Law; he expounds it. Let there be no mistake! He declares: "Don't imagine I have come to abolish the Law or the Prophets! I haven't come to abolish them but rather to make sure they are kept" (5:17).* He then continues:

> For I'm telling you for sure: until heaven and earth pass away, not one letter, not one stroke of a letter, will pass from the law until all is done. 19 So, anyone breaks one of the least of these commandments, and teaches others to do the same, will be called least in the kingdom of heaven; but anyone who does them and teaches them will be called great in the kingdom of heaven. 20 For I tell you, unless your righteousness exceeds that of the scribes and Pharisees, you will never enter the kingdom of heaven. (Matt 5:18–20)*

These might sound like general statements, but they are addressed to the disciples, and they would only make sense if there were some disciples in Matthew's day who were indeed not keeping the commandments. Reading the rest of the Sermon on the Mount, we can see that Matthew was not having Jesus worried about minor matters but about major ones, so that those he has Jesus go on to elaborate in what follows, namely, how to handle anger, sexual desire, marriage, oaths, desire for revenge, and one's enemies (5:21–48). The consistent theme running through these is that one needs to take responsibility to do what is loving. There can be no room for abuse and violence.

That Matthew has disciples of his day in mind who claim the status of being believers and even try to win others, but fail to love, is clear from the way he brings the speech to an end. He has Jesus declare:

> Not everyone who says to me, "Lord, Lord," will enter the kingdom of heaven, but only one who does the will of my Father in heaven. 22 On that day many will say to me, "Lord, Lord, did we not prophesy in your name, and cast out demons in your name, and do many deeds of power in your name?" 23 Then I will declare to them, "I never knew you; go away from me, you evildoers." (Matt 7:21–23)

Even preaching and performing exorcisms in Jesus' name count for nothing if there is no evidence of the love of which Matthew has had Jesus speak. That is the fruit that matters, and just before this warning he declares:

> Beware of false prophets, who come to you in sheep's clothing but inwardly are ravenous wolves. 16 You will know them by their fruits. Are grapes gathered from thorns, or figs from thistles? 17 In the same way, every good tree bears good fruit, but the bad tree bears bad fruit. 18 A good tree cannot bear bad fruit, nor can a bad tree bear good fruit. 19 Every tree that does not bear good fruit is cut down and thrown into the fire. 20 Thus you will know them by their fruits. (Matt 7:15–20)

That goes a lot further than challenging those who rest on the fact that they are "saved" and go on their way. It targets those engaged in religious activity including doing some good. For what counts, according to Matthew, is opening oneself to love and being loving.

The opening words of the Sermon on the Mount reflect what according to Matthew was central for Jesus. There he addresses human need and declares that God's love will bring blessed relief to the poor and broken, those who hunger for justice for themselves and others, those who face grief (5:3-6). These are all promises for the heart filled with love and hope. Matthew was fully aware that religious enthusiasm, even evangelism to win people to hail Jesus, can miss the point. Jesus' priority, according to Matthew, was not to recruit admirers and have others do the same for him, but to embody God's love. His commission to his disciples as the risen one was not win admirers but to make disciples who will learn what they have learned.

> And Jesus came and said to them, "All authority in heaven and on earth has been given to me. 19 Go therefore and make disciples of all nations, baptizing them in the name of the Father and of the Son and of the Holy Spirit, 20 and teaching them to obey everything that I have commanded you. And remember, I am with you always, to the end of the age." (Matt 28:18-20)

Matthew's second major speech addresses the disciples, dealing with the prospect that they, too, would face rejection, even within their families (10:5-42). The third speech reworks Mark's chapter on parables and adds one about the issue of whether to weed a wheat field or just leave it, probably an encouragement to people in Matthew's day not to be judgmental despite much not being right in faith communities (13:1-53). The fourth speech similarly deals with problems within the community (18:1-35).

In the fifth and final speech Matthew returns to challenge believers who seemed happy just to be "saved" and were resistant to opening themselves to love and its consequences (24:1—25:46). Matthew had already had Jesus give a parable that he tweaked to address the problem. The parable of the wedding feast (22:1-14) was originally a confrontation with those who really should have recognized and responded to the gospel and who didn't—while the so-called outsiders did. In Matthew's version it ends with a twist. At the feast of the "saved" is someone not wearing the right garments. That is a symbol of not exhibiting the fruit of an ongoing relationship with God. He is confronted and condemned.

In this final speech Matthew uses Mark 13 in Matthew 24, but then adds three parables in Matthew 25, all three of which address the problem of status Christians, people who would have claimed that they were "saved" but had not opened themselves to the transforming power of love. In the first they are the girls who have not kept their torches burning (25:1–12). In the second they are represented by the slave who simply buried the talent entrusted to him instead of putting it to work, an image of the power of money and investment to depict the power of love (25:13–30). In the final image of the judgement scene, of the sheep and the goats, the focus is on who showed the fruits of love (25:31–46). The sheep were people who engaged in love towards the members of their community. The king, an image of Jesus the judge, declares:

> I was hungry and you gave me food, I was thirsty and you gave me something to drink, I was a stranger and you welcomed me, 36 I was naked and you gave me clothing, I was sick and you took care of me, I was in prison and you visited me. (Matt 25:35–36)

The goats were those, also calling Jesus "Lord," who did not do these things and are condemned. Having had one's sins forgiven, claiming to be "saved" in that sense, counted for nothing if there was not an ongoing relationship that expressed itself in being open to love and loving. Matthew often tweaked what on the lips of Jesus had been a confrontational saying addressed to his contemporaries and their refusal to open themselves to the gospel, so that in his Gospel it became a challenge to members of his faith community who claimed the status of being saved and belonging but who had not embraced the transforming power of love in and through their lives.

COPING WITH ACCEPTANCE

Just as coping with rejection was a problem, so also was coping with acceptance. The challenge of the gospel was to let oneself be loved and to engage in an ongoing relationship with God that made you God's partner in being loved and in sharing love for others. Inevitably, for those who had learned to compensate for lack of love from others and also lack of love for their true self by creating a false self to win love from others, the gospel was a challenge. Mark has Jesus declare that the way to life is to give up such strategies and to embrace the values that Jesus represents and which are the heart of God and therefore of the gospel. Resistance to being loved in this way may vary from distancing to outright rejection and hate.

It was above all Paul who helped deepen our understanding of the way such love worked, including of how it freed people to be loving towards others and so fulfill and indeed exceed what the commandments demanded. Contrasting the closed self as "the flesh," with the open self, embracing the Spirit, Paul highlighted how love bore its own fruit in people's lives, the fruit of the Spirit.

Clearly the assumption throughout is that the gospel is about more than just forgiveness of sins, but then and now it is possible to reduce it to the simplicity of a pardon which guarantees one will be exempt from the horror of hell in the life to come. Sometimes this limited understanding of the gospel leads not to an experience of being loved and valued, but to a sense that how I truly am won't be counted, leaving lack of self-love alive and well.

Matthew takes such limited understandings of the gospel head-on by shaping Jesus' teaching so that it leaves no room for discipleship of this kind. It is like he is saying: yes, a wedding is important, but what really counts is the ongoing marriage and its health. Without it the wedding counts for nothing. And so, Matthew had Jesus' final words make it very clear that what counts is an ongoing life of love, not whether one once had a conversion or even if one called Jesus, "Lord," and became his recruiter.

Telling people off for refusing to open themselves to love is no way forward. "Oughts" are not enough. It would be easy to take Matthew's preference for warning of judgement and seek to frighten people to change. But helping people to see what they are doing in creating their false self requires the gentleness of love to accompany the exposure of its folly. The loss of self-love may run deep and reach far back in time. While for some, some in-depth therapy may be the best path forward, it is a mistake to imagine that such archaeology of the soul is the only way to proceed. Each experience of allowing oneself to be loved for who you are is an exercise in catch-up. At their best, faith communities provide a context where love is both celebrated and expressed in word and deed. Every new experience of love helps set the soul free and helps release it to bear love towards others.

Concluding Reflections

How do you deal with the disappointment you feel when you offer something you cherish, and you want others to cherish, but they reject your offer? How do you cope with someone rejecting your view? How do you cope with dissent?

People's responses vary. They may range from "I hate you! Why don't you love me?!" to disparagement and denigration. At worst, you may embrace the hatred that generates violence and war. At best, you may engage with the other to understand and accept difference and embrace diversity with respect.

New Testament authors reflect various ways of dealing with the disappointment that arose when the early members of the Jesus movement proclaimed good news only to be met with rejection. This would have been especially acute when they were Jews addressing fellow Jews and facing their rejection. It would also have been felt deeply by those who had surrendered their gentile religious loyalties to become converts to Judaism. Even those gentiles who converted directly to the Jesus movement would have needed to confront the fact they had embraced a new faith claiming to represent the faith of ancient Israel, and now found some if not most Jews rejecting their faith.

Hurt, anger, and disappointment would have engulfed some, while others may have brushed rejection aside. But all needed to come to terms with such rejection. In this book we began by exploring such responses. Some, such as those reported of Jesus himself, reflect acceptance that rejections would be inevitable, not least in promoting hope for change, and engage with criticisms by argument. We see this in the anecdotes portraying Jesus' countering criticisms with pithy responses that challenge assumptions.

We also find evidence of efforts to come to terms with such rejections and dissent by exploring why. They included identifying pressures such as persecution and the seductions of the day. It would have been important to have assurance that one was on track and, far from abandoning Israel's faith, was embracing its ongoing story. Telling the stories of Jesus in ways that echoed events of Israel's past was one way of doing so. Another was to present images of divine approval, like the heavenly voice at Jesus' baptism and his transfiguration, as well as to highlight his miraculous powers, a strategy employed also by other would-be influencers of the time, from charismatic teachers to emperors, to enhance their propaganda.

One of the other ways, already well-practiced by other Jewish splinter groups, was to develop a stronger sense of one's own identity, especially as elect or chosen by God and a sense of the identity of the other as therefore not elect or chosen by God. Theistic determinism then dealt with dissent by claiming that it was not only inevitable but meant to be, in the sense of being predetermined by God. Those who dissent or reject are not chosen or elect.

Some might have taken comfort in seeing those rejecting as destined to do so and also as destined to spend eternity in the fires of hell, a descent from hurt to hate. Matthew's employment of the threat of judgement to motivate change lent itself to such use and, at worst, could generate images of God as engaging in acts so easily to be seen as violent and vengeful, sufficient then for the perversity of people claiming warrant for their own violence when they see themselves as in the right, with God as their model.

Such rationales for rejection, deeming some destined for salvation and others not, when pressed for analysis, would seem to require that those destined to reject should therefore bear no blame. But that is not assumed and, indeed, the assumption is usually present that people may change their mind and accept, perhaps even be persuaded by such rhetoric. In other words, what seemed like a closed system was far from that. It leaked.

Concluding Reflections

Some even went even further to portray those rejecting as not just bad because they did so, but bad people in the first place, accounting for their refusal to come to the light. Denigrating those who dissent in this way also went along with declaring those who reject to be children of the devil. Such moves, generated amid a largely inner-Jewish conflict, when taken out of context, developed a life of their own and fed antisemitism, a shameful legacy with its roots in Christian tradition in some of the less healthy ways they coped with rejection.

Another strategy was to gain reassurance from the claim that you alone possessed the way to salvation, embracing an exclusivity that claimed a monopoly in matters of salvation. Applied in the Fourth Gospel, it redrew the image of John the Baptist to remove his offer of forgiveness, but applied in contexts where Jesus' death was hailed as the one and only measure to effect forgiveness and reconciliation with God, it unwittingly disenfranchises also the earthly Jesus, as well as Israel's faith in a forgiving God. Claims to monopoly made missional marketing easier, but at great cost.

Beside these less healthy responses, we visited the way Paul, the apostle, dealt with the rejection, which, as he tells us, he felt very deeply. He, too, could apply the rhetoric of divine predestination and even defend its inconsistencies, but as his final resolution he asserts a mystery of love. He cannot imagine that God would finally abandon Israel. Love prevails in his thinking, at least in relation to Israel, even when he is at a loss to explain how.

We also noted the challenge that Matthew has Jesus bring in the Sermon on the Mount, that truly to do God's will is to say no not just to murder in one's deeds, but also to murder in one's thoughts, hateful anger, and to love not just those who love you, but also those who reject you, your enemies. Stories of Jesus abound with evidence that in God's name, he reached out not just to the righteous but to the least loveable, blatant sinners, with the offer of a relationship of love and forgiveness. And he defended his action by parables that appealed to the best of human care and kindness.

Another element in the gospel of the emerging Jesus movement was the crucifixion of its founder. On the one hand, his resurrection reversed any sense that he was seriously off track. It was a vindication by God, depicted in imagery that belonged to the intense expectations of the time. On the other hand, the resurrection did not remove the sense of the shamefulness of his death. How could such a movement wanting to make its mark in Rome's world have at its heart someone crucified by Rome? We see such concern reflected in the varied retellings of the story of Jesus' trial, which reflect attempts to absolve Rome or at least to depict Pilate as failing Rome, and sadly depicting Jewish leadership as bearing more and more guilt.

Resurrection, therefore, did not remove the need to come to terms with this major event of rejection at the heart of faith. Already Jesus, himself, must have reckoned with the prospect of rejection and execution, not least as he persisted in bringing his message of hope and change to the seat of power in the region, Jerusalem. Since he was acting like a prophet, a prophet's fate would have awaited him. Reports linking him with the dangerous hopes for a Messiah will have sealed his fate. He fitted the category of subversive even if by power of word rather than sword. Inevitably, those who told the story of his rejection, his execution, employed images of the suffering righteous in the psalms, especially Psalm 22, to fill out the story.

We also noted a reversal from what might have been expected, namely seeing Jesus' death as an injustice, a disaster, to seeing it as a blessing. It is likely that some of this revisioning goes back to Jesus himself. We can speculate that behind his actions with the bread and wine in his last meal, now reworked to provide the model for what became the Eucharist, were comments that Jesus must have made in which he saw his death not as defeat but as able to achieve something.

Precedents in the time of the Maccabees and in Isaiah 53 suggested the possibility that death might also achieve blessing. The idea expanded to an assertion that what, in concert with John the Baptist, he had acclaimed in his ministry was now also achieved by his death: forgiveness of sins. Subsequent elaborations could focus on it as a turning point and hail it a saving event. Literal

Concluding Reflections

extrapolations could and do pervert it into an image of God and Jesus that subverted the gospel and portrayed God as not a God of love reaching out, but a God of vengeance who required punishment and retribution before contemplating making an exception by offering love and forgiveness or at least as caring enough to sacrifice his son to an awful death to settle the debt.

Such extrapolations, which subvert the gospel, are, like the misreadings of the language of predestination, a misunderstanding and misreading of religious language. We see this reflected in the fact that in the Gospels such interpretations of Jesus' death as mediating forgiveness stand beside traditions that have Jesus declare God's forgiveness already during his ministry. And John the Baptist, at least in the case of Mark, does the same. These were different ways of conveying the forgiveness that also belonged as core to Israel's faith.

Our final chapter reviewed the challenge, equally difficult for some, then and now, of accepting love. Mark has Jesus challenge the constructions of self that seek to compensate for lack of self-love by winning it from others, a self he has Jesus identify as a preoccupation of the disciples and that he challenges them to abandon. This is neither Jesus' way nor God's way, and Mark employs royal imagery subversively to depict Jesus enthroned on a cross and crowned with a crown of thorns, an image designed to subvert the sad pretensions and strategies of the false self and ideals of personhood as power over others.

Paul's insights into such strategies, which he depicts as the strategies of "the flesh," shows how such strategies produce negative outcomes for others and for the person. His solution is not to demand alternative behavior, but to invite people to be open to the saving grace of the Spirit, which can begin to meet that lost self with love and free it from guilt and fear to be able to bear the fruits of love. The absurdity of the cross is that in its weakness it exercises the transforming power of love that both heals the soul and helps people become good news for their world.

We also considered another way of keeping love at bay, namely reducing the gospel to an offer of pardon, which in effect guaranteed entry into heaven and escape from hell, with no strings attached. Jesus, accordingly, achieved cover for the soul, which remained unlovable and unloved except by proxy. God knows I am unworthy and in myself not lovable, but Jesus covered for me, so I shall escape. Such reduction allows no place for an ongoing relationship with God and walking with the Spirit of love to enjoy and bear the fruits of love, but instead becomes a means of holding it at bay. "Please don't love me! Just acquit me and let me be!"

We saw that Matthew, in particular, challenges such notions, as one might say a wedding counts for nothing without an ongoing marriage. His fantasy of judgement day shows that what counts is a life lived in relationship with the God of love that shows itself also in loving others. Matthew also shows that this is about much more than understanding the meaning of the commandments and keeping them. It is about ongoing discipleship.

Looking at how the first generations dealt with rejection and acceptance, we see healthy patterns and unhealthy patterns. The options then have remained alive through history, making Christian faith a bearer both of harm and of health to our world. It has inspired some to be happy to write some people off, even to hate, indeed, even to sanction violence and see this modeled by God. It has also inspired others to engage difference with love, talk through difference by argument, but never let sadness and hurt degenerate to hate, and to see this modeled in God.

The world then and the world today needs the love that is at the heart of the gospel, that can help heal the unloved soul, help free it for love and help model that love in the way we deal with conflict, difference, and diversity.

www.ingramcontent.com/pod-product-compliance
Lightning Source LLC
Chambersburg PA
CBHW032233080426
42735CB00008B/839